Think Like A CEO

Stop reacting, get out of your own head and take control of your role

BYRON MORRISON

Byron Morrison books may be purchased for educational, business, or sales promotional use. For information, please email byron@byronmorrison.com.

First published 2021.

First edition.

Designed and edited by Iulia Protesaru.

Contents

A note from the author

This book is a great starting point in helping you master the mental game needed to be a highly effective CEO.

Does this sound like the situation you're in right now?

- You're feeling stretched thin, overloaded and overwhelmed by everything that needs to get done
- You have so many competing priorities that you often get stuck spinning your wheels or doing tasks that don't lead to growth
- You're highly reactive and a lot of your days are spent putting out fires and dealing with other people's problems
- You get times where you overthink, second guess yourself, struggle making decisions and procrastinate, avoiding what you know you need to do
- You're not clearly communicating, setting expectations or keeping people accountable
- You struggle with balance and even when you do take time off you're attached to phone thinking about work

If this sounds like you, then I'd love to take a moment to talk to you about how beyond this book I can help you get this under control.

I developed the Evolved program for CEOs who want to become more effective in their role. Using my battle-tested 5-step Evolved Method, I want to evolve you into the CEO your business needs to break through to the next level of success.

Working directly with me, I'll help you change the way you think, how you process problems, navigate challenges, manage people and perform in your role. By the end, you'll be able to maximize your time, lead with confidence and grow a business without losing your sanity.

Just a few of the things we'll do include:

- Figure out what you need to prioritize then implement the right processes to effectively delegate, manage your workload, defend your time and maximize what you can get done

- Up-level your leadership skills to improve how you handle tough conversations, communicate expectations, bring out the best in your team and hold people accountable

- Break through the mental blocks that cause you to procrastinate, overthink and doubt yourself, so that you can consistently take the actions you need to take

- Get you out of a reactive state so that you can stop, process problems and calmly respond to them, allowing you to feel more in control with less stress and anxiety

- Develop the right habits and routines to help you feel energized, stay focused, manage stress and feel your best inside and out

- Implement 'Ideal Life Creation' so that you can find balance, switch off, put the right boundaries in place and enjoy the success you worked so hard for

This is how I'm going to help you take control of your life and business, so that you can become the leader your business needs to take it to the next level of success.

The Evolved Method has been implemented by CEOs in 18 different countries by CEOs running everything from tech to SAAS and AI companies, real estate businesses, 7-figure agencies, financial institutions and billion-dollar unicorns in Silicon Valley.

Here's what a few of my clients had to say about the process:

Cole (CEO): *"When something so transformative or someone so transformative enters your life it's really hard to put that impact in words right and that's that's how I felt about this entire experience working with you...As a Founder as a CEO as a person I could not more highly recommend working with Byron because it'll change your life, it's as simple as that. It couldn't be more of an honor or a pleasure to be able to call him a coach, a mentor a friend and a person you won't meet many people if any people in your life who are better human beings than this man is. So thank you Byron for everything that you've done everything you continue to do."*

Ron (CEO): *"After working with Byron and him offering the tools and rewiring my mindset, I have now come back as a more confident leader, I have learned how to defend my schedule, I've learned how to be less reactive, but to also to be able to just pause and look at situations and come up with a better plan, a better solution. I've set new standards...and I'm very confident that Byron is going to change your life for the better".*

Jordan (CEO): *"When I first started working with Byron, I really didn't feel like I was where I wanted to be. I felt like things were out of control, I didn't know how to get my life of working 80 hours and was struggling to spend enough time with my family. I was really trying to get that back, and what I found was that so much of what I didn't feel in control of, I had the ability to get in control of by changing the way I thought about things, by changing the way I approached situations, how present I was, having a true vision for my future, having action plan that really allowed me to recapture that control, to get organised, to come into meetings and be with my family, everything improved."*

Max (Tech CEO): *"Honestly, it's been one of the best decisions I've made. Certainly, compared to the financial investment the value that's come out of it has been astounding."*

Tyler (Business owner): *"I feel like I've left this universe and gone into a different one. It's been incredible...If you judge my level of happiness, clarity, sleep cycle, relationships, confidence, or every other area of my life, it's an easy win. My direction in life has completely changed".*

Rosemary (Business leader): *"I don't feel like I have control back, I feel like I have it for the first time. I used to be fighting all these fires and battles and it was exhausting. As everything felt out of my control and I was miserable. Now I feel calm and like that fire is merely a distraction that I know I can handle."*

Michael (CEO): *"I've gone from completely tired, exhausted, drained to back to my old self so to speak and with more purpose. I'm glad I did it, I certainly know that if I didn't, I'd probably still be in that state of unhappiness and stress. It was the best money I've ever spent on myself".*

Neil (Business owner): "*I now feel completely different, I feel clear-headed and able to focus on the stuff I work out that I should be focusing on, I don't jump around anywhere near as much...I'm in control".*

Lauren (CEO): "*You said you'd make me a better leader and you did. The time we've spent has been invaluable and our sessions are always exactly what I need to calibrate and process problems*".

Josh (Business leader): "*People around me recognised that I'm more effective than I've ever been*".

Are you next?

Joining is by application only, to discuss next steps get in touch at **byron@byronmorrison.com**
Find out more and apply at:
https://www.byronmorrison.com/evolved-program

Before you get started:

Before you dive into this book, there are two actions to take that will accelerate your progress and amplify your results.

Action 1: Download the Resources

Included with this book are various bonuses, guides and resources to help you on this journey.

These bonuses have been specifically included to help you take what you learn and implement it at the next level.

They include “The Effective CEO Planner”, “The CEO Time Audit Process Training” and “How To Plan As An Effective CEO”. These trainings will show you how to properly plan and structure your days to ensure you can maximize your time and perform at the highest level.

You’ll also get access to “The Impact Driven CEOs” Facebook community where I’ll be doing live Q&As, you can meet other CEOs, exchange ideas and get support on this journey.

Because of that, before going any further download and access to them at:

https://www.byronmorrison.com/book-resources

Action 2: Connect on social

I have a YouTube channel and a series called "The Effective CEO". On here you'll find videos covering everything from figuring out what to delegate and prioritize to ways to defend your time, decision-making frameworks, energy management strategies, habits of highly effective CEOs, planning your day and so much more.

Watch them now at **https://www.youtube.com/@ByronMorrison**

Every day on social media I share videos, posts and content diving further into what it takes to become a highly effective CEO.

You can also connect with me and follow my content at:

LinkedIn:
https://www.linkedin.com/in/authorbyronmorrison/

Facebook:
https://www.facebook.com/byronmorrisonauthor/

Instagram
https://www.instagram.com/authorbyronmorrison

You can also join the "Impact Driven CEOs" Community, where you can exchange ideas, meet other CEOs and get help with challenges at:

https://www.facebook.com/groups/impactdrivenceos

Introduction

In 1969 Laurence J. Peter published a book called the "*Peter Principle*" where he talked about how "every employee tends to rise to his level of incompetence." Now, I'm sure we can all think of people who do well, get promoted, and then either never go any further, or who crash and burn.

While the book was satire, it garnered a lot of attention and even led to various studies. One being a study by scientists from the Carlson School of Management on salespeople being promoted. They were surprised to see that "the best salespeople were becoming the worst sales managers". The findings uncovered that this happened because even though they may have been great in their expertise in sales, they knew nothing about managing others, leading a team, or making management level decisions. Meaning that the reason why they struggled, was despite their ability to thrive in their role, the skillset simply wasn't transferable (or in many cases even applicable) to the next.

In my work with CEOs, I see the "Peter Principle" all the time. Regardless as to whether it's a founder whose expertise has helped them grow the business, or someone who has worked their way up the ranks to step into the role...

Suddenly they find themselves in a situation where on top of focusing on growth, they also need to lead a team, keep stakeholders happy, pitch to investors and overlook the day-to-day operations. It's a huge amount to stack on top, which is why understandably they can feel out of their depth in a sink or swim situation. And it's usually at this point when the "Peter Principle" kicks in.

That's why do you know what the biggest bottleneck in most businesses is?

I'll give you a clue. It's not the wrong strategy, issues hiring the right team, or even poor market conditions.

Instead, the biggest bottleneck in most businesses...

Is the CEO.

Because when they aren't performing at the level they need to, decisions don't get made, projects get stalled, opportunities get lost and the business falls apart. The reason why this happens is because they're trying to handle new levels of problems with an old level of thinking. Which in turn, causes them to get stuck in their own head, overthink key decisions and spend their days feeling stretched thin and overwhelmed.

To put it another way for you, think of it like your old laptop.

Remember how when you got it, it worked great? It was fast and could handle everything you needed it to?

Yet after a while, remember how it started to slow down? Its memory wasn't as good as it used to be? It had difficulty handling multiple tasks at once? And if you put too much pressure on it, it would crash and stop working?

What most people don't realize, is our brains work in the same way. And this goes back to the original point Laurence J. Peter was trying to make. As the reality is that in life and business, we can only get so far with our current level of thinking and actions until we hit our own level of incompetence. Because of that, the level of thinking that got these CEOs to where they are, simply isn't enough to handle the challenges that come with this new level of success. And it's the exact reason why they become the bottleneck.

These shortcomings go a long way in contributing to the fact that after the first year in business, 50% of businesses go bust. And after ten years, only 4% survive. Meaning that 96 out of 100 businesses simply aren't going to make it.

Because of that, if you want to give yourself the best possible chance to succeed, then your business has to be able to change. It has to be able to innovate. And it has to be able to persevere. Who drives that change? It's you. Which is why you need to master the mental game that comes with being an effective CEO, adapting and evolving along the way.

Now in my experience, there are generally two types of CEOs in this world.

On the one side, you have the overwhelmed CEO. They're spending their days bouncing around from one thing to the next, feeling stretched thin, overthinking, struggling to make decisions, second-guessing themselves and on a rollercoaster ride of ups and downs. And because they're so pulled into day-to-day problems, they're struggling to find the time or bandwidth to focus on tasks that drive the business forward.

On the other side, you have the Evolved CEO. They're laser-focused and possess radical confidence, unshakeable emotional resolve and the belief within themselves that no matter the challenge, they can handle it and get through. Because they feel in control of their role, they show up powerfully each and every day, they don't make decisions from a place of fear and they're able to consistently operate at the highest level.

The difference between the two is the Evolved CEO recognized that their business growth will never outgrow their inner growth. This is why they invested in the support, time, and energy needed to raise their level of incompetence and create the inner growth needed to take themselves and their business to the next level.

Which raises the question - how exactly do you create that inner growth?

Going back to the old laptop example...you upgrade...you evolve your way of thinking.

Which brings us to the purpose of this book.

Because here's the reality - the mindset required to be a founder, entrepreneur or manager is vastly different to that of being an effective CEO, and in many ways the behaviours, thoughts and beliefs that once served you, may now be holding you back. That's why in our time together I'm going to be showing you how you can evolve your way of thinking, so that you can stop reacting, get out of your own head and make decisions like a CEO. By the end of this book, you'll have a new perspective on what it takes to be a highly effective CEO, and you'll be able to take that mentality and use it to propel yourself forward in everything that you do.

Now just to be clear, when I say this book is about mindset, you're not going to be finding some generic advice to meditate or some super zen spiritual practices inspired by Tibetan monks. Sure, those practices have their place, and they can have a huge impact on your mental wellbeing and longevity. However, this book is all about adopting the mindset to navigate organizational challenges, align short-term priorities with long-term targets, deal with setbacks, effectively communicate and leverage the time of those around you.

Along the way, I'll also be sharing real-world CEO case studies and unique perspectives I've gained from 1000s of conversations with CEOs and business leaders behind closed doors. Showing you the teachings in action and how you can implement them yourself. Now this is key, as it is in the implementation that you will create the greatest results in taking control of your role.

As your guide in this journey, one thing I want to make clear – I'm not a business coach and it's not my job or my place to tell you how to run your company. So if you've come here looking for some fancy growth hacks or strategies to scale your business, then you're in the wrong place.

If anything, for what we'll be covering your business is actually irrelevant, as we're going to be taking our focus away from the business and instead placing it on you. Diving into how you're showing up and what it really takes to get you to perform at a higher level.

What I find time and time again with clients though is that once you get this right and you evolve within yourself, that growth directly impacts the business as well. And it's often the catalyst needed to break through to that next level of impact, income and success. After all, your mindset is the glue that holds everything else you do together.

Now, I know that "mindset" is hardly the sexiest of ideas and it's often the last thing most people want to spend time on or invest in. Even though it's generally the biggest thing holding them back and what they need the most. That's why I'm so excited that you're here, as you reading this right now already shows you're starting to think differently and recognizing what's actually important.

With that being said, to get the most out of this book my challenge to you is to take some time at the end of each chapter to reflect on what you've learned. Think about how it applies to your own life, where you can implement the teachings and how you can follow through with this way of thinking. Also set aside some time to do the tasks and fully embrace what you discover, because if you do, this will be the turning point in your performance as a CEO or leader.

I know you're no doubt inundated with self-proclaimed "gurus" and thought leaders promising miracle solutions if you follow their secret to success. Which is why before we go any further, I think it's important to tell you a little bit more about myself and my journey, as that story will set the context of everything else that we'll be covering.

About the author

In case you're new to following me, my name's Byron Morrison. I'm a mindset and high-performance strategist, speaker, and best-selling author.

What I do is help CEOs take control of their role by evolving them into a more confident, grounded and effective decision-making leader, who can handle the pressures of running and growing a company. How? By taking their mindset, emotional control and performance to the next level.

All this started after my dad's cancer and seeing the pain and suffering he went through during his treatment (including spending 25 days in ICU, most of which was spent on life support and breathing through a tracheostomy). That experience set me out on my own journey of transformation, where after losing over 50 pounds and turning my life around I took everything I learned and it became the foundation of my first best-selling book 'Become a Better You'. Off the back of that, I grew a company helping people from around the world to live healthier, happier lives.

While I was great at the delivery aspect, truth be told, I was completely in over my head when it came to running a company. After all, I'd never managed a team, dealt with so many competing priorities, made huge decisions or had to balance all this with continuing to drive growth. As a result, I found myself stretched thin and overwhelmed by everything that needed to get done.

My solution, was to keep pushing and to cram more into my days, as with so much going on I was convinced that I couldn't slow down. Inevitably, I found myself burnt out and exhausted, with a feeling of dread every time I looked at my calendar and saw the fire that I had to face next. It was consuming, and even when I did take time off I was attached to my phone or thinking about work. I was there physically, but mentally I was checked out, causing a huge amount of disconnect in my relationships and happiness. So much so, that I reached a point where I started to question whether or not this was actually worth it. I didn't want to just throw in the towel, so I made a decision that I had to figure out how to get this under control.

To make that happen I became a student of everything from mindset to managing people, dealing with conflicts, high performance and how to be an effective leader. Reading books, getting coached, mentored and everything I could to figure out how I could become the CEO my business needed. And it worked, I was able to finally get off the rollercoaster ride of ups and downs and start showing up as my best self in everything I did. Not only did this allow us to continue growing, it also meant that I was finally able to impact more people all while creating a life of freedom on my terms.

Looking back, it's now clear to see that the mental and emotional drain had been causing me to be nowhere near as effective as I needed to be as the leader in my business. This is why I now realize that the biggest barrier in the way of our growth, had been me. My tendency to overthink decisions, second-guess myself or avoid the actions I needed to take had caused me to become the bottleneck. By changing the way I thought, processed problems, empowered those around me and navigated challenges though, that's how I was able to get out of the way so that we could break through to the next level of success.

From the clients I was working with, I saw I wasn't alone in feeling this way. At the time I was working with a lot of CEOs and business leaders on their health and naturally as we discussed what was draining their energy and impacting their well-being these challenges came up. This helped me discover that supporting others to navigate these problems was not only my superpower, it was also what I loved to do. This is why the natural evolution of my work was to help other CEOs and leaders who feel overwhelmed by the challenges that come with their growth to get them under control.

Since then, I've been fortunate to work with CEOs and business leaders in 15 countries. An experience that has allowed me to deal with problems and challenges behind closed doors that very few people in the world will ever have been exposed to or even be aware are happening. What this allows me to do is bring a unique set of insights, perspectives and ideas to the work that I do, to help others overcome what is standing in their way. All of this allowed me to discover that for someone to reach their potential, there are three core pillars they need to master: mindset, emotional control and performance.

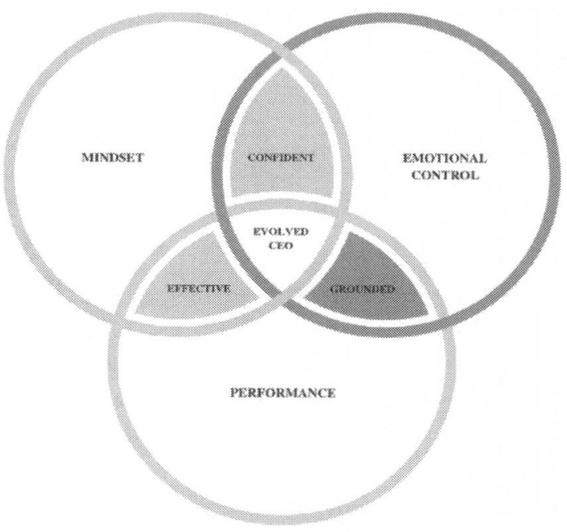

This is how they get the clear head focus to make better decisions, the confidence to execute without overthinking and the emotional control needed to handle the pressures of running a business.
I'll be coming back to this later in the book when we focus on what it takes to break through to the next level.

From that discovery and my subsequent work, I developed a proven five-step process to help CEOs and business leaders evolve within themselves to create the radical confidence, unshakeable emotional control and amplified effectiveness they need to take back control of their life and business. Which is why whether it's been through my books, coaching, consulting, or speaking, my work has been focused on using my unique method to help others handle the challenges that come with their success.

My first book in this series was *"The Effective CEO"*, which primarily focused on the performance aspect, showing you how to hone your focus, prioritize your time and consistently perform at the highest level.

And as you probably guessed from the title...this book will primarily be focusing on mindset and showing you how to think, lead and make decisions like a CEO. However, as they are so closely related, we will also be pulling in elements of the emotional control side of your role, as well dipping into performance.

If you have any questions or want to know more about anything covered in this book, get in touch using the email below and I'll personally respond. **byron@byronmorrison.com**

Now that we've got the overview and introductions done, let's get started.

Section 1

Stop Reacting

The problem for most overwhelmed CEOs is that most of their days are spent in a state of reaction, where everything they do is a response to the challenge in front of them. And this is a huge issue, as they can be so focused on immediate problems that they become stuck in the trenches, where their days become all about just getting through. This in turn, can keep them focusing on short-term issues, leaving them without the time or bandwidth to focus on tasks that drive the business forward.

I see this all the time in new clients who come to me for help, where inevitably they find themselves going through the motions, with the rollercoaster of running a business feeling like a huge mental and emotional drain. I've been there myself, which is why I know how frustrating and exhausting it can be. Especially when you're falling short of the impact, income and freedom you know you could create.

Going back to what we spoke about in the introduction, the level of thinking, actions and behaviours that got you to where you are, isn't going to be sufficient in handling the new level of challenges that come with your success. Let alone help you break through to the next level.

That's why if you want to be an Evolved CEO, you simply can't afford to think like a manager, founder, or entrepreneur. After all, their attention will often by design be short-sighted, focused on a singular area of the business, dealing with immediate problems and trying to please those around them. Yet as an Evolved CEO, you simply have to act differently, know when to let go of responsibilities, trust those around you and make choices others couldn't even comprehend.

I saw this in a conversation with a client who is still fairly new to the CEO role. He felt like he needed to be present with his employees, walking the production floor and making himself available. Now, this is an extremely admirable trait, but what tended to happen was that every time he went out, people would bombard him with what was wrong and expect him to solve their problems. Even if they had nothing to do with him or the business – like fixing a broken car window. Because of this action, it meant that distractions and fires were taking up hours of his day, consuming his bandwidth to the point that the majority of his time was being spent trying to make other people happy. Not only was this frustrating, it was also exhausting.

When we dived into the issue deeper, I uncovered that the reason behind this mental barrier was he didn't want people to perceive him as lazy or locking himself away in his ivory tower. That was why he felt like it was important to keep up appearances and portray an image that he was "busy", even though it was taking him away from being productive. While he could have gotten away with this back when he was a manager, now he simply couldn't afford to allow it to consume his days. After all, he was promoted to CEO for a reason, which was why he needed to focus on driving the business forward and the responsibilities that could only be done by him.

Does that mean he could never walk the floor and engage with employees? Of course not, but we needed to set boundaries, reserving these tasks for allocated periods around his high-value work (work that has the greatest impact on the business and that can only be done by him) and ensuring the time was limited to an hour, rather than those reactive problems taking up most of his day.

If you want to become an Evolved CEO, then you have to be able to balance your focus between small and big picture priorities, leverage the time of those around you, get out of your own head and effectively navigate challenges thrown your way. That's how you take control and it's exactly what this book is all about.

Before we can do any of that though, we need to get you out of that state of reaction. Because if you let your emotions get the better of you or you crumble under pressure, then the harsh reality is you simply will not succeed. That's why we need to make you aware of your responses and to take back control of how you think, feel and react. Because until you get that right, nothing else matters.

Controlling the controllable

This is the foundation of the work I've done with clients for the last few years, which is why I've seen time and time again that this isn't just important for how you perform as a CEO, and instead, this will directly influence every area of your life. In fact, this and this alone will directly contribute to everything from your mental state to your ability to handle challenging situations, how you bounce back from setbacks, breakthrough procrastination and ultimately create results in your life.

Now if you've been into personal development for any period of time, you've probably encountered some of the concepts in this first chapter before. But here's the thing - if you know it, but you aren't doing it, then you don't actually know it. That's why I don't want you to skip ahead or brush this off, as in order to ensure you take action, I'll be giving you some tasks to help you apply what you learn and follow through.

With that in mind, there are three things I'm going to teach you in this section that will allow you to start shifting to the mindset of an Evolved CEO. The first of which is...

Step 1: Cause and effect

In life you're either at cause, or you're at effect. There's no middle ground. This is why people will learn what I'm about to share with you, say it makes sense and move on, but if they don't actively embody it, it doesn't work. Once you take this on and you ingrain it within your awareness, it'll completely transform your way of thinking. That's why the first step in this journey together is getting you to move from effect, to cause.

When I talk about being at effect, what I mean is allowing outside forces, whether it's other people, your environment, the past, the situation you're in or your problems to dictate how you think, feel, react or behave.

I'll give you a few examples.

Let's say you're working on a project and a member of your team makes a mistake and your response is to get frustrated or lose your temper. That's you being at the effect of them and what they did.

Or you have a huge board meeting and in anticipation of tough questioning you find yourself getting anxious and overwhelmed. That's you being at the effect of the situation.

Or you want to post a video on social media for your marketing or do a talk, but you're scared of what other people will say or think so you avoid it. That's you being at the effect of others and their judgement.

Or you want to go for a run, but then it starts pouring with rain. So instead of going to a gym, working out at home, or even just facing the rain, you sit on the couch eating Doritos and watching Netflix. That's you being at the effect of the weather.

The problem with all of these situations is that you're not empowering yourself and instead, you're allowing something outside of your control to dictate how you think, feel, react and behave.

This is key, because while most people live their life being at the effect of the world around them, as a CEO looking for long-term prosperity, you simply can't afford to allow yourself to be governed by your emotions. Especially since the problem with being at effect is that it keeps you trapped in your own head, focusing on the past, what went wrong, or what is out of your control. Which as a result, is what keeps you procrastinating, fearing failure, controlled by your emotions and ultimately, this is what is stopping you from performing at the level you could or need to.

That's why being at effect is related to every other area of this book, and it's why before anything else will work, you have to get this right. Here's what you need to remember:

Whether it's in life or business, as much as you wish otherwise, you are never going to be in complete control of what's going on around you.

What's the one thing you can always control though?

How you choose to respond to it.

In fact, this is so important I'm going to say it again and highlight it...

You are never going to be in complete control of what's going on around you, but the one thing you can always control is how you choose to respond to it.

Like the example I gave of getting frustrated or snapping at your team. In that moment, your reaction is at complete effect of what has happened. Whereas if you were at cause, you could've stopped, processed what was going on and instead of being dictated by your emotions, chosen how you respond.

Getting this shift really is what makes the difference between the Evolved CEO who has the calm headed composure to perform at the highest level and the overwhelmed CEO who falls apart anytime something doesn't go their way.

In fact, we see this happen in sport all the time, where the entire game is on the line and the athlete steps up to the plate a nervous wreck. Completely at the effect of the situation, allowing the pressure to take its toll and crumbling, forever going down in history as the person who couldn't cut it when it mattered most. Whereas the elite athletes who keep their cool, filtering out the stakes and what's going on around them, embracing the situation and focusing on what they can do about it...They're the ones who knock it out the park.

The mindset of an Evolved CEO is no different to that of an elite athlete. After all, running a business is like an endurance event, filled with ups, downs, challenges and setbacks. It takes extreme perseverance, years of hard work and a commitment that very few people will ever realize or understand. Which is why your mindset and ability to be at cause or effect, is what will make or break your success.

In its simplest form, it all comes down to being responsible for your own actions, thoughts and reactions. While this may not be its true definition, if we take the word responsible and break it down, we get "response-able". As in, you are able to choose how you respond.

That's why if you have something you need to do, whether it's in your role, relationship, for your health or anything else in your life, who is the only person who has the responsibility to do it?

Obviously, the answer is you, and if you responded differently, you'd be at effect.

Which is why ultimately, who is responsible for getting results in your life? Again, it's you.

Once you realize that, take ownership and decide to give up being at the effect of the world around you, that's when you'll become unstoppable.

One really important thing to remember is that there is no middle ground for cause and effect. Because whenever you're at effect, you're not empowering yourself and it will continue stopping you from making the right decisions, taking the right actions, or showing up as the best version of yourself. Now, I'm definitely not saying this is easy, but if you want to gain the ability to deal with any situation or solve any problem, then you have to be totally at cause for the majority of the time. Does this mean you'll no longer get frustrated, have moments of anger or procrastination? Of course not, after all, you're only human. But what matters most is how you empower yourself and how quickly you take back control in those challenging times.

For instance, before one of my private clients started working with me, he had a tendency for setbacks to spiral to the point that he'd shut down, unable to regain his focus and be knocked out of the game for days at a time. All because he was completely at effect, focusing on what he couldn't control and allowing it to push him over the edge. After the work we did together and he implemented what I'm sharing with you in this book, he reached a point where he could put himself at cause, regain his composure and shake it off in a matter of minutes. Shifting his entire mindset to one which could move the whole company forward. At the end of this section, I'll give you some tasks to fully apply what I'm taking you through, so that you too can do the same.

One thing I need to reiterate is that when I say you need to take responsibility, whether it's for your reactions, decisions, or actions, it's never about blame. And this is key, as when you start blaming yourself for what's happening, that's when you fall into focusing on the past, beating yourself up and being hard on yourself. The reality is though, you can't change the past. What's done is done, which is why instead this is all about taking responsibility for how you respond and what you do about it going forward.

One of my CEO clients is a perfect example of someone who was stuck in this trap. Whenever something went wrong, she'd land up beating herself up, blaming herself for what happened and fixating on what went wrong. She was completely at the effect of the past, whereas the reality is that no amount of blame is ever going to undo what happened. Because of that, our focus had to be on shifting her mindset from the past, to the future and taking responsibility for what she needed to do to take back control.

To put this into perspective, take a moment to think of a problem or challenge that's causing you frustration, stress, or anxiety right now. Maybe it's with a member of your team dropping the ball with a client, a mistake that was made on a project, a conversation you've been putting off, a task you've been avoiding, or something you did wrong that you're beating yourself up over.

Got one?

Now, you have two choices. You can either choose to continue focusing on what went wrong, feeling guilty or wasting time and energy on something you can't change. Or you can focus on the present and what you're going to do about it going forward. Because just think, what action do you need to take? What do you need to do to let this go? What could you do that even though it may not magically solve the issue, would be a step in the right direction?

Either way, the problem is the same, but the way in which you choose to look at it is completely different. Because of that, your actions and results will be completely different as well. Notice how I said "choose". Because if you want to think like a CEO, you have to take a step back, look at the bigger picture and not allow yourself to get drawn into the past. This shift in itself is huge, as while one perspective will keep you stuck, the other will empower you and allow you to move on, propelling you towards your goals.

Am I saying to simply dismiss and ignore mistakes? Of course not, but instead it's all about learning from them and focusing on what you're going to do about them.

And look, I get it. Sometimes you can give something your all, putting your blood, sweat and tears into your goals, yet still come up short. I've been there so many times myself, where it feels like you're giving your business everything, and still things keep going wrong. So there's no point in sugar-coating it, as in these moments you can feel completely deflated, where it takes everything inside of you to pick yourself up and keep going. That's why I truly believe you have to be a special kind of crazy to be a CEO and sign up for this life (that goes for entrepreneurs and business owners as well). After all, it can feel like a never-ending battle, where every day you're getting punched in the gut, only to have to get up smiling and come back for more. What you always need to remember though, is you chose to sign up for this life. Not only that, but it's meant to be hard. As if it was easy, it would make for a pretty boring autobiography.

That's why your ability to master the mental game of being a CEO and put yourself at cause, even when it feels like everything is going against you, is what will truly determine your ability to persevere. You've probably heard the saying "fail fast, learn fast", and this is where I like to add my own extra step: "choose to move forward". As even when setbacks arise or things do go wrong, it's on you to focus on what you can control and how you're going to regain momentum.

In fact, this is why whenever clients come into sessions dwelling on the past or complaining about what happened, my favourite question to ask them is – "what do you need to do about this?"

For instance, on a call, one of my clients was really beating himself up over a funding contract they didn't get. Now, let's be honest, the situation sucked, and it was a huge blow to their momentum. With that being said though, it's how the hand played out and no amount of dwelling over what happened was going to change it. That's why when I'm working with clients as much as I can empathise, it's not my job to throw them a pity party or console them. Instead, it's on me to pick them up, to refocus their attention and find ways to turn lemons into lemonade so that they can move forward. One of my clients said to me it's amazing how positive I am and how I can turn these perspectives around. It's not because I view the world as all sunshine and rainbows, but instead, it's because I know allowing someone to focus on the past or remain in that negative state is never going to serve them. And instead, regardless of the setback, it's always about shifting their focus to what they're going to do about it going forward. For the client who lost the big contract, that meant figuring out what he needed to do. What new opportunities they could pursue. And what other paths this setback opened up.

Remember, setbacks are inevitable, it's part of the game and they come with the territory. That's why whenever something goes wrong, those simple words "what do I need to do about this?" can be so empowering. After all, even in the biggest setbacks lies opportunity. You'll never see it though if all you do is focus on what's wrong.

A big part of adopting this mindset is recognizing that in life you're not always going to have caused your problems. They might be down to factors completely out of your control, something you went through, the actions of others, or even due to beliefs and fears you took on when you were younger. But until you stop allowing yourself to be at the effect of them, they will forever hold you back.

One of my CEO clients is a perfect example of this. When we first met, he was in the stages of growing a tech company and in doing so he was looking at taking on a team. This was causing a huge bout of imposter syndrome, as he worried he wouldn't be a great leader or be able to inspire those around him. When we started breaking down this belief, we uncovered it went all the way back to the start of his career, where he had a complete disaster in leading a team on a project. As we started to unpack it further, we uncovered that despite his best efforts, the infighting and toxic environment meant he had been unable to get that team on the same page. An experience which had led him to take on a belief that he wasn't a good leader. A story that was now ingrained within his head.

Over the last few years though he had numerous situations that proved otherwise, where he'd led others to great results and incredible wins. Yet despite that, subconsciously he was still being at the effect of the past, going back to that one time he failed and overlooking all the times he succeeded. It was only when we brought that to light that he could change how he viewed himself and his own capabilities.

Not only that, but even though they may be frustrating or incredibly painful, it is often in our failures and mistakes that we learn the greatest lessons and create the biggest growth. Which is why these setbacks in our past are only a bad thing if we don't learn from them. Like with this client, that experience had taught him how to better handle toxic environments, what to look out for when hiring the right team and the exact culture he wanted to avoid creating. Which was why for him, it was actually a huge positive. Yet because he was so focused on his perception of how that first experience played out, he completely overlooked all the positives he gained from the struggle he went through. Once we flipped his perspective though (which we'll be coming back to later in this book), he was able to set himself free.

In your own life you'll have been exposed to environments, experiences, situations, people and events that have, for better or worse, shaped your mould of the world. Can you see from all of this how they can ingrain beliefs within you? The problem with beliefs is that often you don't even know that they're there, as they're just played out as stories in your head. Because of that, we have to get to the root cause of why this has happened, recognizing why you took on the belief and the lessons you need to learn from it to let it go. It's important to note, the lessons you need to learn have to be positive and they have to be about the future, otherwise they will keep you trapped in the past.

Breaking through this on your own can be a challenge. Especially since we tend to get stuck in a tunnel vision of what's going on around us. Which is why breaking through these beliefs may require having someone else to help you shift your perspectives and fully see what's going on. However, a useful exercise you can do is to take some time to journal and map out what beliefs are currently holding you back. Really think about where you doubt yourself, fear putting yourself out there or hold yourself back. And from there, ask yourself – when did I decide this? What happened for me to take on this belief? And what do I need to learn from this to let it go and move forward?

Just to reiterate, whether it's from your past or what happens to you throughout the day, being at effect is whenever you allow something outside of your control to determine the way you think, feel, behave, or react. Whereas being at cause is whenever you take responsibility for your actions, decisions, reactions, or emotions. Because of that, no change is going to come until you recognize where and when you're being at effect, and you place yourself at cause for how to deal with it going forward.

I'll share some tasks with you to do exactly that shortly, but for now, I want to ensure that you understand all this.

With that in mind, do you get what being at cause and effect is all about? And do you see how being at effect directly impacts how you think, feel, react and behave in every area of your life?

That's step number one, cause and effect...

Step 2: Focusing on what you want, not what you don't want

This seems really simple. After all, just scroll through your newsfeed and it probably won't take long until you stumble across some motivational fluff post saying something like "energy goes where focus flows". Yet despite people thinking they know this, they still get caught up focusing on what they don't want.

The reason being is if you go back thousands of years to the days of cavemen, the entire basis of life was to survive. A good day would be to find some food, a nice cave to sleep in and not get eaten by some wild beast. Yet even though society has changed and evolved since then, subconsciously, we're still wired in exactly the same way. Just turn on the news and everything you see is terrorism, death and destruction. All playing into our primal instincts to look out for and respond to danger. The problem with always focusing on danger though, is it causes you to focus on what you don't want. And when you focus on what you don't want, you attract more of it.

I'm not going to go into the full science behind all this, as honestly, it would be completely unnecessary for you to know. But just as an overview, right now there are millions of things going on around you, from the feel of your shirt on your body to the taste in your mouth, smells and sounds. If your brain tried to process them all it would explode (not literally but you get what I mean). So instead, what happens is it generalizes and sorts it based on what it recognizes is important to you, breaking it down into small bits of information and then using that to create the lens in which you view the world.

It's important to note that this lens can change depending on what you focus on. For instance, have you ever thought about buying a new car, and all of a sudden you start seeing it everywhere? Or you buy a new shirt, and other people are wearing it? It's not that it wasn't there before, you just didn't notice it because it wasn't important to you. Which was why your mind simply filtered it out and generalized it. Once it comes into your awareness though, your mind actively looks out for these items and scenarios.

The reason you need to be aware of this, is because this is an unconscious process, meaning we don't even realize it's constantly happening throughout the day. That's why it's so important to take responsibility for focusing on what you want, not what you don't want, because if you don't, you'll continue getting stuck in your own head.

If you've ever felt anxious, you'll know what I'm talking about. Where in that state you keep saying to yourself "I don't want to be anxious, I don't want to be anxious, I don't want to be anxious". So, what happens? All of that anxious energy continues to build up inside you and you become even more anxious.

This was a huge struggle for one of my CEO clients. When we first met his business was going through a round of funding, which meant he needed to do pitches and presentations to secure investment. Yet in a presentation a few weeks prior, he completely froze under tough questioning, losing his train of thought and as a result, bombing the pitch. The experience made him feel completely anxious about all his upcoming meetings, to the point that the thought alone was having an almost paralyzing effect. The problem was he was focused on the past and what went wrong, that it was causing him to fear that the same thing would happen again. Like I said to you before though, when you focus on something, that's what you get more of. This was why he was ending up in a self-fulfilling prophecy, where his fears, thoughts and actions would all come into alignment and he'd shut down, reinforcing the belief he couldn't do presentations. That's why we needed to shift his focus from what went wrong, to the times he succeeded, his passion and expertize. Along with mentally going through how he was going to handle the situation. Visualizing how he wanted to show up, the way he wanted to present himself, the presentation he wanted to deliver. The result? By shifting his focus from the past to the present, he was able to go into the next pitch and crush it. Giving him a new level of confidence in his own abilities and what he could do for the company's growth.

That's why it's so important to remind yourself that your past doesn't have to define your future and just because something happened once, doesn't mean it'll happen again. Instead, all those failures and setbacks are simply stepping stones, preparing you to succeed.

This is also a perfect example of how you can start to see how important language is, especially when it comes to how you speak to yourself. Because if you end up using negative language traps (more on them shortly) you'll continue going round in circles, where you'll try to focus on what you want, but not actually believe or act on it. Now, I know that what I've shared with you so far are simple principles. However, these are the start of you creating momentum and taking back control.

Can you see how if you don't get this right, problems will continue to manifest and keep you stuck? Once you take responsibility for putting yourself at cause and focusing on what you want though, then the final step is to...

Step 3: Take action

What I've taken you through and the reason why this works, is any time you need to take action you can mentally go through this 3-step process. Whether it's breaking through procrastination, facing that challenging conversation, speaking up in that meeting, or even pushing yourself to go to the gym, the same process you need to follow to create results will be putting yourself at cause, focusing on what you want and taking action. As with anything else, things are always easier when you have a process to follow. And chances are that a large majority of the problems in your life and business right now could probably be solved by you acting on them.

The problem is that when you're stuck in effect, you get stuck focusing on all the reasons not to do something, and the longer you leave it, the worse it becomes. Think of it like a bungee jumper standing on top of a cliff. The longer they stand there, the harder it becomes to jump, as the fear continues to build up inside them until they feel paralysed. Whereas they could immediately solve that problem by jumping.

And for you, it's exactly the same. Whether it's a difficult conversation you need to have, project you need to start, call you need to make, workout you need to do, or the launch you need to put out there...like the bungee jumper, the longer you delay, the more the fear will build up inside you and the worse it will become.

Is facing it going to magically make the entire problem go away? Probably not, as there will be further actions you need to take from there. But facing the problem is the first step, especially since you're probably going to need to face it eventually anyway. Meaning that the longer you delay, the more you'll allow all that negative energy to build up inside you, taking up focus and bandwidth that could be put to better use. By pushing yourself to take action though, you can immediately solve the initial problem, removing the hold it has over you.

It's like when one of my clients first came to me, he had a huge tendency to avoid confrontation and difficult conversations. So much so, that he'd often avoid them for weeks, if not months at a time. He even had a staff member he wanted to fire for over six months, but he just couldn't bring himself to face that conversation. Not only was his inaction hugely detrimental to the business, it was also taking up a huge amount of bandwidth due to him worrying and feeling guilty over what he was avoiding.

Once he put himself at cause for what he needed to do, focused on what he wanted and took action, he got it over. As a side effect, by pulling off the band-aid he realized that it was nowhere near as bad as he initially thought it would be. This in turn made him more confident in handling these situations and future events became easier to face. It's even reached the point now where if he knows he needs to do something, he either does it immediately, or he schedules it for the earliest possible time, as he's realized that the sooner he gets it over with the better.

That's why focus is pointless if you don't do anything with it. And this is why so many people in personal development get stuck. After all, it's exciting to map out your goals and design that fancy vision board of all the things you want...the reality is though that you can focus on what you want till you're blue in the face, but if you don't take action, then it's irrelevant.

This is one of the biggest differences between overwhelmed and Evolved CEOs. While overwhelmed CEOs avoid uncomfortable situations, work on tasks they feel like instead of what they should be doing, or talk about their goals but never do anything about them...Evolved CEOs push themselves to take action, as they know that's what determines their results.

Not only that, but putting it on hold actually takes more energy than just getting it over with. We've all been there, where you sit around procrastinating over what you know you need to do. Sometimes for 8, 10, 12 hours. It's exhausting and by the end of the day it leaves you feeling worse than if you'd spent the day digging ditches.

The worst part though, is that often once you start that task you quickly get into the zone, or you realize it isn't that bad and didn't take that long. Yet all the time you wasted caused unnecessary stress and overwhelm that could have been avoided.

This doesn't just apply to responsibilities in your business. It's like when you cook dinner and you know you need to clean the kitchen. But you really don't feel like it, so you sit on the couch trying to relax and telling yourself you'll do it later. What happens though? It stays in the back of your mind, so instead of enjoying your evening, you keep thinking about what you need to do. Whereas if you had put yourself at cause, focused on what you needed to do and pushed yourself to take action to get it done, you would've solved the problem and been able to relax.

It's the same for whenever you're procrastinating over starting that report, facing that difficult conversation, or even mustering the motivation to exercise. All putting it off does is further amplify the problem, all while adding the guilt and beating yourself up that comes along with it. Because of that, if you want to think like a CEO, then you need to make a decision to put yourself at cause, to focus on what you want and to take action. Especially if it feels uncomfortable. That's how you build momentum. You lead by example. You push forward and make progress.

Like I said, knowing this and actually following through with it are two very different stories, which is why I've got three tasks to help you implement what I've just shared with you. Not only will these make you more aware of how you think, feel, behave and react, they'll also create a huge shift in putting you back in control of your life and business.

Task 1: Removing negative language traps

You may have noticed so far how big of an impact the language you use and how you speak to yourself can have on your focus, actions, beliefs and whether you're at cause or effect. That's why task 1 is all about removing the negative language traps that cause you to get stuck in your own head. On the outside, this may seem overly simple, but what you'll see is that by recognizing, avoiding and removing these words and phrases you'll be able to transform how you think, view problems and the results you can create.

Negative language trap 1: "this makes me that"

"She makes me angry."
"What he's doing makes me so frustrated."
"The rain makes me sad."
"This meeting makes me anxious."

"Makes me" implies that someone or something can make you feel or behave a particular way. Remember back to cause and effect, as you have the ability to choose how you respond to any given situation. Meaning that even though it may not always feel like it, the way you feel and react is always completely under your control.

For example, let's say a member of your team does something that makes you angry. The reality is they haven't made you angry, instead, you are choosing to get angry because of what they did.

Whenever I speak to someone who is stuck in the world of effect, they'll defend this to the death, putting the blame on others and avoiding taking responsibility for how they react. Defending their emotional response and blaming their reaction on someone else. Regardless, it doesn't make it any less true.

A prime example of this is road rage. You know when you're driving down the road and a car pulls in front of you, so you start swearing and shouting, telling them they're an idiot and they don't know how to drive? Even though that reaction is on impulse and it feels out of your control, you're being at the effect of that situation and allowing it to dictate your response. Worst of all though, that other driver is going to drive off and go about their day, yet for so many people, that triggering event is then something they carry with them, taking it into everything else they do that day.

Another example of being at the effect of what's going on around you is a situation I found myself in a few months ago. I remember sitting on a train and across from me was a group of kids who were shouting and screaming. I remember just sitting there on the edge of my seat, getting beyond frustrated that they wouldn't shut up and calm down. In that moment I realized, I was completely at effect. As they weren't annoying me, and instead, I was choosing to get annoyed by what they were doing. After all, if I put myself at cause, then there were so many solutions to my problem. I could turn up my music, focus on something outside the window, get back to work, or even move seats. Yet because I was so fixated on the problem, I completely overlooked all the alternatives, instead focusing on how they were "making me" annoyed. Once I realized that, centred and grounded myself, I could shift my focus and let it go.

Because of that, it's vital to recognize that no one can "make" you anything. Once you become aware of that, you can completely alter your mood, reactions, and responses. For instance, going back to the example of "she makes me angry", let's say a member of your team makes a mistake and you lose your temper. In that moment, it's vital to stop, mentally take a step back and remind yourself that the situation isn't making you angry, you're choosing to get angry because of what has happened. That simple mental conversation in itself can at times allow you to refocus, gain perspective and shift your response. Not only that, that shift will also allow you to see the situation and your feelings for what they truly are, and from there what you can do to control them.

It's important to note though that breaking away from being at effect isn't going to make you immune to reactions or emotions. Instead, it's about you having the self-awareness to recognize how and why you feel a particular way. After all, sometimes just being in tune with yourself and in the moment becoming aware of how and why you feel a certain way, can be exactly what you need to take back control. That's why in these times of heightened emotions, it's essential you recognize what's happening and put yourself at cause to change your response (we'll dive more into that in task 2).

Negative language trap 2: "hope"

"I hope I can do this."
"I hope I can get to the gym later."
"I hope I get these results."

With "hope" you're essentially saying that you're hoping the stars are going to align, the planets are going to come together and everything is going to magically work out for you. Putting your results into external factors and implying that you have little to no effect on the outcome.

It's like going into a diet saying "I hope I can lose some weight". Meaning instead of taking responsibility to eat healthier and exercise, you're putting the results in some external force and saying they're out of your control. Giving yourself an excuse and justification before you even fail. That's why instead, it's essential to shift your focus to the actions you need to take to create the results you want.

One thing I need to point out with "hope", is that obviously, there are exceptions. As let's say you've done everything you can on a proposal or pitch to a new client and now the outcome is out of your hands. Obviously if you say you "hope you get it", in this context, you're not at effect, as there is nothing more you can do to influence the outcome. Instead, "hope" is only a negative language trap if it has something to do with an outcome or action within your control.

Negative language trap 3: "try"

Like Yoda said in Star Wars, "do or do not, there is no try".

The problem with the word "try", is that often you put the outcome on your future self, hoping they get it right. Like when someone asks you to go to an event, but you don't really want to go. Instead of saying no, you say "I'll try and make it". What's happening in this moment is that you're essentially hoping that either your future self will get the motivation to go, or you'll think of an excuse. And if you don't go, you can then justify not making it because at least you had said you'd "try".

I used to do this all the time when I was first attempting to get in shape. Telling myself "I'll try and go to the gym later". When really, deep down I was hoping something would come up, so I wouldn't have to go.

To make matters worse, this causes all that negative energy to build up inside you. As you keep thinking about it, feeling guilty or wishing it wasn't a problem. That's why if you want to think like a CEO, it's vital that you don't allow your focus or bandwidth to be taken up by these problems. That means, stop saying you're going to "try". Instead, take that pressure off yourself by making a decision and committing to it one way or the other. Because if you really don't want to do something, then just say no.

Negative language trap 4: "if"

"If I get this right."
"If I stick to this plan."
"If I can finish early on Thursday we'll go for dinner."

“If” implies that getting results is out of your control and it keeps you in a world of effect. That’s why you need to change “if” to “when”.

Not only will changing this one small word put you at cause, mentally it completely changes your focus. Creating a new belief and determination that you not only can, but you will get results.

I saw this on a client call where the CEO has various challenges he needs to navigate as they focus on scaling and making several huge transitions within the business. When we first met, he would second-guess himself at every turn, having huge issues in trusting his convictions or believing in his own capabilities. Yet through the work we did and him mastering what I’m sharing with you in this book, on a recent call he effortless stated “when I get this right”. I pointed that out to him, as I know 12 months ago he definitely wouldn’t have had that certainty. Yet now not only did I believe every word he said, he believed it as well. A mindset that in turn will make him unstoppable with what needs to get done.

It’s important to note though, that he only got that shift in the way he thinks because he committed to doing the work and implementing the tasks I’m sharing with you now.

Negative language trap 5: “should”

We’ve all got things in our life we feel like we “should” do.

“I should read more books.”
“I should go to bed on time.”
“I should get some exercise.”

The problem with the word “should” is there’s no feeling of urgency or necessity. So again, it ends up in the world of “hope” and “try”, where it’s easy to get dismissed or forgotten about. Whereas when you have something in your life you "must" do, you find a way, regardless of what's going on.

This in itself is why it's so vital you have an honest conversation with yourself about what you actually want. Because if you keep saying you "should" do something, but don't, then feel bad about it, then a deeper question to ask yourself is why? Why can't I commit to this? And when I don't, why do I feel bad about not doing it?

After all, it's easy to tell yourself you should do something just because you feel like it's expected of you, or because it's what you should be doing. But if you don't truly want it, then stop putting that pressure on yourself and let it go. On the other side though, if you truly want something but keep putting it off, then it's vital you change that "should" to a "must". Because here's the thing, if you want to live a life of the 1%, then you simply have to hold yourself to a higher standard. That means pushing yourself to take control of what you want and not wasting time on what isn't serving you or adding to your life.

I find that a lot of the time our "should" is driven by being at the effect of something else. One of my clients was a prime example, as she kept telling me "I should post more content online to grow my business". Yet whenever it came to it, she'd make an excuse or put it off. When we got deeper, we uncovered that the reason why she was avoiding putting out videos was she had a deep fear of being judged. But once she decided that she wasn't going to let the opinions of others hold her back from what she needed to do, she was finally able to overcome that fear. As a result, she's now regularly posting content, spreading her message and reaping the rewards of a growing business because of it.

Whether you need to get started on that report, launch that new project, hit the gym, or get to bed on time, that change in focus may be exactly what you need to follow through. Let's use exercise as an easy to follow example. When you change that "should" to a “must” and you focus on all the reasons why you need to do it, it completely shifts your perspective, and ultimately, will transform your actions and results.

This may seem simple, but the reality is that one single shift in a word can completely change your perspective and how you look at the situation you’re in. Meaning that once you stop using the words “makes me”, “hope”, “try”, “if” and “should”, you can shift your perspective and start changing your mould of the world.

Because of that, I want you to teach this to someone else. It could be your partner, a friend, or someone else you speak to on a regular basis. Say to them “whenever you hear me say these words, I want you to call me out on it”. Doing so will help you start developing the awareness of how often you say them, which will go a long way in enabling you to change your response.

This is also one of my favourite things to do with clients, as I find that about three weeks into the process, they catch themselves as soon as these words come out of their mouths. Immediately saying “I’m at effect” before I can even point it out. With that in mind, you won’t get this right straight away, and that’s ok. The goal of this is not perfection, and instead, it’s about developing your awareness and changing the way you think.

One thing I can guarantee is that from now in conversations, whenever someone is complaining, making excuses, or justifying why something can’t be done you’ll pick up on these negative language traps. You’ll also start to see exactly why that person is stuck and why they’re not getting results.

Task 2: Taking back control

Task 2 is all about developing your awareness about when and why you're at cause or effect, along with actively empowering yourself to create the results you desire.

In order to do this, throughout the day whenever you find yourself being at effect, stop, take a deep breath, imagine mentally taking a step back, and ask yourself "why am I being at effect?" "What's causing me to feel this way?"

What this will do is force you to detach yourself from the situation, so instead of getting caught up in the moment, you can bring into your awareness what is actually going on and why you're in a heightened or emotional state. As maybe you're getting frustrated over a mistake that was made, overwhelmed by an upcoming meeting, or procrastinating over a project you need to start. Rather than allowing the emotions to spiral, stop, ground yourself, figure out what is happening and then ask yourself "how can I empower myself? What action do I need to take? What can I do about this?"

On the other side of this, at times when you do feel at your best, you're in a state of flow and bringing your A-game, do exactly the same thing. Stop and ask yourself what have I done to put myself at cause? How am I empowering myself right now? How can I sustain this momentum, or repeat this mindset in the future?

Doing this is going to go a long way in helping you recognize how and why you think, feel, react and behave the way that you do. In turn, that awareness will allow you to create a shift within yourself, where you can start to control your responses and behaviours throughout the day.

The importance of breathing

The reason why forcing yourself to stop and breathe is so important is that when you're stressed your blood pressure goes up, cortisol spikes and you can't think clearly. This will explain why in this heightened state you get brain fog, don't make the best decisions, or perform properly.

To make matters worse, often this is compounded, as all of the stress throughout the day causes tension to build up inside you. Think of it like a gas tank, where every challenge, setback or difficult situation continues filling it up, till eventually it can't take anymore, and it explodes. This will explain why situations that in isolation wouldn't have mattered can push you over the edge.

I saw this with a new client who kept acting on impulse and making emotional decisions she would later regret. By making this simple change, she managed to regain her composure and in a recent session she said to me that once she took a step back, she realized a lot of these problems weren't actually a big deal – especially once she took a moment to process them, detach from her emotions and fully understand what was going on.

That's why before taking any action, by forcing yourself to stop and take some deep breaths, you'll be able to lower your heart rate and blood pressure, ground yourself, regain your ability to think clearly and put yourself in a far better position to act. This is also why I recommend to all of my clients that at the end of every big task, situation or focus point throughout the day, they stop what they're doing and use a breathing tool I call "The Stress De-Compounding Technique".

"The Stress De-Compounding Technique"

I originally got this idea from a practice taught to A&E doctors and nurses in the NHS (the British health service) to deal with crisis situations. In those moments, it's normal for adrenaline, panic and stress to kick in, which is why it's vital they calm down before making decisions or taking action. While different scenarios, the response to dealing with fires for CEOs can in many ways trigger the same response. That's why I tested a tweaked concept out on myself and then with clients, and it was so effective, it became a staple tool in the arsenal of my Evolved program ever since.

To do this, stop what you're doing, if possible close your eyes, and from there, take a deep breath in to the count of four, then out to the count of four. In to the count of four, then out to the count of four.

Focus on your breathing and imagine that with every exhale, you're letting go and pushing out the tension built up inside of you.

You want to continue doing this for anything from 60 to 120 seconds, however, I've found the sweet spot generally tends to be about 90 seconds. Just listen to your own body, as when you feel calm and grounded, that's an indicator that you're ready to stop.

I highly advise adding this action into your routine so that you can release tension after every big task and at regular intervals throughout the day. By doing so, you'll notice a huge difference in everything from your focus to your stress levels, how you handle pressure and the control you have over your emotions. Not only that, but do you know how some days you look at the clock and you're exhausted, yet it's not even 3pm? That again can be linked to all that built-up tension, which is why this simple action to release tension can completely transform your energy levels and performance as well. Again, this is all about thinking like a CEO and implementing little shifts and changes that are going to give you an edge. When you add them all together, it will completely transform your ability to show up at your best every single day.

Stop, notice, observe

The big takeaway here and one thing I always advise clients is to never take action or make decisions when you're at effect, as you'll rarely do so as the best version of yourself.

For instance, one of my clients was bombarded by fires over email every single day. In a perfect world we would have limited how often he checked his inbox, but unfortunately with his role, he needed to keep on top of customer issues. The problem though was that every time an email popped up it would spike his stress levels, and often he'd respond immediately based on emotion, rather than how he would if he was calm and composed. Meaning he'd regularly overlook something, miss word his response, or be so quick to reply that he'd miss out parts of what needed to be said. He'd then have to then follow up again shortly after to fix his mistake, leading to even more stress, frustration and wasted time.

That's why we implemented a new process where after reading a stressful email, he'd take a moment to stop, close his eyes, take some deep breaths, and only once he was calm would he type out his response. To take it a step further for really important emails or issues, he committed to not sending the response for 15 minutes. This gave him time to step away, gather his thoughts and then go back and ensure his response said everything it needed to say.

Now I need to add that while on paper this sounds easy, for him it was a huge internal battle, as he needed to overcome the belief that everything needed an immediate response. While it felt uncomfortable, once he saw that the building didn't burn down if he didn't instantly reply, he felt far more at ease in making this shift. That's why it's important to note that many of these changes may cause internal tension, especially if they go against your ingrained behaviours or how you've always done things. In which case, you will just need to persevere, reminding yourself that these actions are no longer serving you and that you need to break the hold they have over you.

Again, this is all about thinking like a CEO - a grounded leader and an experienced problem solver. Understanding why you feel a particular way and controlling what you can control is the key to getting there. Often this can be done by stopping, taking deep breaths until you feel calm, then asking yourself why you're at effect and what you need to do to empower yourself.

Sometimes though, the best thing to do is to change your environment. After all, when you stay in the place that is creating the stress, it can cause tension to continue to build up, making it even hard to regain your composure or let it go.

I saw this challenge as a reoccurring issue with one of my clients. As part of her role, she was spending most of her days chasing managers and working on reports. A responsibility that meant she was constantly bouncing around from one task to the next and stressing over everything that needed to get done. When things inevitably started going wrong (which with that moving parts they always did), her response was to try and work harder to push through. All that did though was cause her to become even more overwhelmed, as all that built-up tension made it impossible for her to think clearly and eventually, it would have an almost paralysing effect. At times the brain fog would get so bad, that she'd read a paragraph of a report, then feel completely blank, unable to remember what she read. Meaning she'd then have to read it several more times just to make sense of what was happening. In turn, this would cause tasks that should take 20 minutes to take several hours, simply because she was struggling to focus or keep her attention.

Because of that, I pushed her to agree that whenever she started feeling overwhelmed or tension build-up, she had to stand up and walk away. The reason being is that often by removing yourself from that physical space, you can remove the emotions that are tied to it. From there, she was tasked with taking a few minutes to regain her composure, with the agreement that only when she felt grounded could she return to her office and continue working. She was massively reluctant to do this at first, especially since she had so much to get done, that she believed she couldn't spare the time to take a break or step away. But trusting in the process, she reluctantly agreed. As a result, she found that those few minutes away completely transformed her focus, lowered her stress levels and allowed her to remain calm in all the chaos. Because of it, she also massively amplified her productivity and what she was able to get done in a day. The reason being was those few minutes would save her hours of time that was previously being lost in a state of mind that had diminishing returns on what she was doing.

When it comes to stepping away, I've had clients get great shifts by using that time to simply go for a walk, meditate, stop for a coffee, listen to music, or even call a friend. It really doesn't matter, as long as it allows you to release tension and get back to a calm and clear state of mind. This is also why I advise clients to schedule these buffers after activities that they know will have heightened emotions. Let's say you have a board meeting that you know will be intense. The worst thing you can do is take that energy into what you do next. Instead, figure out what calms you down and allow yourself that gap to process how you feel and move on. For one of my clients, this meant making it non-negotiable that after every intense meeting he goes for a short walk to shake it off. For another, he closes his office door and allows himself to meditate and calm down. There really is no right or wrong, and instead, it's all about testing what works for you.

The usual overwhelmed CEO response however is – "I'm too busy and don't have time for that". Yet as a result, rushing back into their day with those heightened emotions massively impacts their focus, productivity and performance. This is why an Evolved CEO is aware of those traps and commits to allowing themselves time to get back in the game, as they recognize those few minutes to recalibrate are vital in ensuring they can continue performing at their best.

It's important to realize, that there are always going to be times that push you over the edge. After all, you're only human, so the work we're doing in this book and beyond isn't about making you immune to your emotions. Instead, it's about getting you to understand and act on them in a way that is under your control, so that you can bounce back as quickly as possible at times you do get derailed.

That's why I encourage my clients to focus on what I call "the 15 minute rule", whenever they're in the thick of it. Essentially, this is giving yourself permission to have 15 minutes to process and deal with what has happened. Now you may want to go for a walk, meditate, take a break, or go through whatever you need internally to process and move through it – with the caveat being that at the end of the 15 minutes you're going to commit to stopping, taking a deep breath, and letting go of whatever negative emotion you're feeling, so that you can focus on what you need to move forward.

You'd be amazed at how big of an impact setting a time limit on dealing with these emotions can have. With one of my clients, as they were a service-based business dealing with hundreds of members daily, he'd regularly get complaints and issues. Yet as he was so passionate about the business and community, he'd often take them to heart, seeing these complaints as a reflection of himself and allowing them to weigh on him for the rest of the day. That's why whenever this happened, instead of allowing himself to dwell all day, he gave himself 15 minutes to process what happened. To go through the emotions, figure out why he was feeling that way and at the end, commit to letting it go. A shift that had a huge impact on not just how he dealt with setbacks, but also how he mentally and emotionally felt every single day.

This action also allowed him to disconnect himself from the situation. In doing so he saw that he felt that way due to the high standard he believed the business was keeping and that in fact, the issues were not a reflection of who he was as a person. Again, a realization he could only have come to by taking the time to stop and process what was going on, instead of just bottling it up and being at the effect of how he felt. By repeating this action, he's now reached the point where he doesn't even need to commit to 15 minutes, as he's able to brush off these complaints in a few short moments.

Sometimes though, life can have a way of truly punching you in the gut. Like when you put everything into that pitch and don't get the funding, where that campaign you thought would take you to the next level bombs, or when you're faced with having to let people go. In these times, I'd take the "15 minute rule" a few steps further. I've found that on days like these, an intense activity may be exactly what you need. Going into that run, gym session, hitting a punching bag or whatever you need, telling yourself you're going to let out all that tension and when you're done, move on. Again, it comes down to what you focus on, the language you use and putting yourself at cause for how you feel. This is what thinking like a CEO is all about, as while most people will spend their lives at the effect of the world around them and carrying that tension into everything they do, you simply can't afford to operate that way. Instead, you need to find ways to pick yourself up, brush it off and keep moving. As it's not just for you, it's for your team, your customers and the impact you want to make.

Alternatively, never underestimate the value in having someone to talk to. I speak to overwhelmed CEOs all the time whose usual tendency is to bottle up stress and internalize how they feel. A behaviour that is not only unhealthy, but also puts a huge mental and emotional strain on them, directly impacting their performance. That's why I believe it's vital to have someone you can talk to and who can create a safe and judgement free space for you to open up about what happened and get it off your chest. I find with clients that one of the most valuable aspects of the work we do is every week just creating an environment where they can verbalize and discuss what happened and how they feel. I don't mean that in a spill your guts kind of way, and instead, sometimes just saying it out loud can be a huge relief in taking the weight off your shoulders. We'll come back to this topic later in this book, but whether it's a therapist, coach or mentor, I highly advise getting someone in your corner so that you don't have to get in the ring alone.

On a final note, it's important to remember that the reality is that the more success you create, the higher the stress and stakes will become. This is why mastering your ability to control your reaction is what will make the difference in you being an overwhelmed CEO and you being able to thrive at the highest level.

I know this isn't easy, but remember, these challenges are part of the role and this is the life you signed up for. This is why you don't just need to think like a CEO, you need to behave like one too. That means putting yourself at cause and acting within your control, even if there is chaos around you.

Task 3: Cultivating internal growth

To further build on the shifts you create, it's vital you actively take time to reflect on what has happened. After all, it is in reflection you'll create the greatest growth, learn the biggest lessons and see the biggest transformation in your performance as a CEO.

That's why your final task at the end of each day is to take a piece of paper and draw two columns. (You can also do this in a spreadsheet, on your phone, or anywhere else that works for you).

On one side write down three things that went wrong and on the other side three things that went right, along with what was your responsibility in making them happen.

This final part is key, as if you just write down what went right and wrong, you don't get anything out of it. This is why the entire purpose of this is getting you to stop and really take in what happened and your contribution towards it. I also find that as humans, we subconsciously tend to only focus on the bad, overlooking or completely dismissing what went right. That's why this exercise is going to force you to put yourself at cause for the good and the bad things in your life, putting the full picture of what's going on into perspective.

A perfect example of this is a coaching session I had on a Friday afternoon, where the client came on the call deflated. When we started breaking down what was happening, he told me about a setback they had with a proposal earlier in the day where a member of his team missed some financial figures off a report. This oversight didn't fully portray the competent image he wanted for this potential client and as a result, he was fixating on what went wrong. Because he was at the effect of the situation and hadn't let it go, he came into our call feeling the week was a complete disaster. However, when I shifted his attention to what else happened that week, he remembered that they secured two new clients, made huge progress on a project, made some massive new hires, and created huge traction in their market. If anything, it was probably the best week ever in their business, yet because he was so focused on this one thing that went wrong, he completely overlooked what went right. When I pulled this into perspective for him, he laughed and said "you're right, it really isn't a big deal" and he let it go – especially since he had already taken action on resolving the problem by sending the potential client the correct figures.

This is also why it's so vital to recognize that as a CEO, your growth and achievement isn't always going to be linked to financial milestones and often there is huge progress to celebrate in other areas. Many of which you'll never notice or be aware of if you don't take regular time to reflect on the journey. And this is key, as most overwhelmed CEOs live in the past or the future. Whereas if you want to think like an Evolved CEO, you have to focus on the present, understanding what's happening and using the clarity you gain to drive you forward. That's why even though this may not be glamorous, and it may at times feel like a chore, I can guarantee that when you regularly take time to reflect, you'll massively reap the benefits.

One thing I need to reiterate though is when you're doing this task, it's never about blame. You're not blaming yourself for what went wrong or beating yourself up over what you did or didn't do. Instead, it's all about uncovering what your responsibility was in making it happen.

For instance, let's say you wasted an hour scrolling through the newsfeed rather than working on that report. Your responsibility was you should have put down your phone and got to work. With that in mind, what can you learn from this that you can do next time? Maybe you need to turn off your phone during work periods, or remove certain apps that can distract you.

Another example is maybe your day got away from you and you got stuck in busy work or fires, which in the grand scheme of things, didn't actually matter. Because of that, a course of action could be to get more organized with your planning, defend your time, or prioritize what needed to get done.

On the other side of this, maybe you needed to have a difficult conversation, so instead of putting it off, you faced it, got to the bottom of a problem and took the first step towards resolving it. Which shows you dealing with these issues sooner rather than avoiding them needs to be your normalized approach.

It's important to note that this doesn't just apply to your role as a CEO, as at times some of your biggest wins or challenges will be outside of work. For instance, maybe you got caught up and once again missed date night. Which in turn is causing problems at home and as a result is affecting your focus at work. Meaning it's your responsibility to set stricter boundaries and prioritize this area of your life. Or on the other side, maybe after a long day despite being tired you pushed yourself to go for a run, as you know doing so will help you sleep and keep you energized. Again, recognize the win and what you did to take responsibility to make the action happen.

It's so key to reflect on your life on the whole, as that will be the only way to figure out where to focus your attention going forward. That's also why regular holistic reflection is so important, as you may find that your problems can be linked to issues you don't even realize are related. For instance, if you're struggling with focus, energy and performance, you may think it's down to a busy week or having too much on your plate. And sure, that could be a factor. But it may also be due to neglecting sleep, not eating properly, problems at home, or a variable in another area of your life. After all, everything you do, how you look after yourself and the daily choices you make will directly impact how you think, feel and perform. Auditing what is going on in every area of your life will be the only way to uncover and focus on the root cause of the problem.

I have the reflection process I just shared with you in place with all of my private clients, where every day for the first two weeks they check-in with me sharing this table (after which we go to a different check-in process Monday to Friday). Not only does this keep them accountable to ensure they follow through, it also allows me to track and keep on top of the challenges they're facing, how they deal with situations and what's going on in their lives. Then every week in our sessions we can break down what happened, the biggest lessons that need to be learned and how they need to deal with them in the future.

The way you can do this yourself is to go back over these reflections, ask yourself what lessons you need to learn, how you can handle similar situations in the future and what you need to do differently the next time. Remember the key thing here is not to dwell on the past or beat yourself up, and instead, it's all about focusing on the future and preparing yourself to better handle these situations the next time you face them.

During our sessions we also take time to future pace what's incoming, looking ahead at the next seven days and figuring out what challenges could come up. By doing so we can create a game plan for how to deal with them, so if and when the challenge happens, instead of reacting, they can proactively revert to the pre-determined response. Again, you can repeat this yourself by setting aside time to look at the week ahead and uncovering what challenges you may face, along with how you need to effectively handle them.

This past and future reflection is the real secret to how true growth, confidence and evolution is created and it's why my Evolved program is able to create such huge transformations in putting CEOs back in control of their roles.

To take it up a notch, what I do with clients is to take a bird's eye overview of their reflections, looking for triggers, correlations and reoccurring problems. By doing so I can study their patterns, looking for psychological loops, triggers and behaviours, which in turn will allow us to see what patterns we need to break. After all, when you have clarity in how you think and what you need, everything comes together. This reflection can go a long way in uncovering red flags or underlying ongoing issues that need to be dealt with, as when thought patterns are out of alignment, that's what causes issues and incongruence. Once you've done this for a few days, go back and see is anything repeating. Maybe whenever you have a difficult meeting your stress levels go up? Maybe a certain task triggers anxiety? Maybe you keep getting frustrated with a certain member of your team?

Again, overwhelmed CEOs just get stuck in the trenches, focused on solving immediate problems, rarely stopping to think about how they handled situations or what they can learn. If you want to think like an Evolved CEO, this regular and continuous reflection is going to be a key factor in your growth. After all, it is in these challenges that you learn the biggest lessons, how to do things differently and you develop the full awareness of what is actually going on.

That's also why it's vital you take this self-imposed pressure off yourself to get everything "perfect". Because at the end of the day, it's never going to happen and fearing achieving anything less than perfection will forever be a mentality that will hold you back. By doing this process, you will improve and every single day you'll get a little better (which compounded over time will be huge).

As for the task itself, I generally get clients to do this every single day for at least two weeks. That way it builds the habit of consistency, and it also gives us enough data and findings to holistically review what's happening inside and outside of their role.

That's why my challenge to you is to commit to doing the exact same thing. This shouldn't take more than a few minutes and to ensure you don't forget, set a reminder on your phone or schedule this in as your final task for the day. I'd also recommend scheduling some time at the end of each week to go back through all your reflections, looking for correlations and the biggest lessons you need to apply. Then at the end of the two weeks you can make a decision on whether or not you want to continue this practice, or move to another form of reflection.

For my clients, I move them to a different check-in system after this time period, one which looks at everything from how they handle situations, to their energy, productivity and performance. In doing so, I can effectively track and monitor how they feel on a day-to-day basis, optimizing accordingly and dealing with underlying problems before they throw them of course. For instance, a run of low energy days could be a sign that we need to address their workload, sleep, stress, or other factors before they crash or burn out.

I don't want to overwhelm you with too much information and tasks at once, so you can download the week three and beyond reflections in the resources pack at:

www.byronmorrison.com/resources

As a recap, here are your tasks for the next 14 days:

1) Remove the negative language traps of "makes me", "hope", "try", "if" and "should".

2) Throughout the day, whenever you find yourself at effect stop, take a deep breath, calm yourself down and mentally take a step back, asking yourself why you're at effect and what you can do to empower yourself.

3) Whenever you find yourself at cause, taking an action you'd normally avoid, in a state of flow or bringing your A-game, do exactly the same thing. Stop, ask yourself what you've done to empower yourself and how you can repeat this in the future.

4) At the end of each day create your reflection table with three things that went right, three things that went wrong, what your responsibility was in making them happen and what you can learn about them.

I know we covered a lot in this first section, so take a little bit of time to reflect on everything and put together a game plan for what you need to do.

If you want to take this a step further and get more direct support to help you take control of your life and business, then feel free to reach out to me at **byron@byronmorrison.com** to see if I can help.

Want to dive into this further?

Check out my YouTube channel and "The Effective CEO" series. On here you'll find videos covering everything from figuring out what to delegate and prioritize to ways to defend your time, decision-making frameworks, energy management strategies, habits of highly effective CEOs, planning your day and so much more.

Watch now at **https://www.youtube.com/@ByronMorrison**

Section 2

Strategic Thinking

If you want to think like a CEO, then one of the most important skill sets you need to develop is the ability to balance long-term thinking with short-term challenges and priorities. Yet this is also the area where the overwhelmed CEOs I speak to struggle the most. After all, it's difficult to see anything beyond the battle if you're stuck in the trenches. Which is why their tendency to get caught up in reactive problems causes them to get stuck in a state of response, where as a result, they're left without the time or bandwidth to focus on tasks that drive the business forward.

As I'm sure you can imagine, this is a huge issue. Because when you're just focused on short-term problems, it can back you into a corner, where you make decisions based on emotion, fear, or only prioritizing immediate challenges. Often these will be short-sighted, at the expense of the bigger picture or what is ultimately best for the business. As the leader of a company, it's vital that you're able to view actions, decisions and problems in their true form, and know when to take risks, when to push and the real implications of your actions (or inactions). As ultimately, it's often the toughest calls or actions based on short-term loss that can lead to the biggest long-term gain.

Yet most people focus on short-term thinking, that in the now satisfaction, or instant gratification, with no consideration for the consequences of their actions. This is how they live 99.9999% of their life, a state of mind that massively hinders their growth personally and professionally.

Probably the best illustration of this is by Ray Dalio in his work where he talks about the "order of consequences". A way of thinking that completely transformed the way I view the choices I make not just in my business, but in every area of my life. In the "order of consequences", Ray states that the first order of consequence is focused on short-term thinking, whereas the second, third, fourth, fifth, are all long-term benefits. Consequently, they have a cost to the first order, often involving sacrifice, discomfort, or pain.

To put it into perspective, I'll use an easy to follow health example.

Gary wants a bar of chocolate, as it makes him feel good when he's had a long day. Making it a first order consequence. Meaning when Gary eats the chocolate, he is momentarily satisfied and feels good. Now if that was the full picture, then that consequence is a good one, as Gary's had his chocolate and he's happy.

However, when we look at the potential second, third, fourth and fifth (long-term consequences) it's a completely different story.

1) Gary who has struggled with his weight most of his life continues gaining weight

2) He loses energy, confidence and belief in himself, causing him to hold himself back and settle in his life

3) He doesn't get the success, fulfilment, or happiness he desires (or deserves)

4) He doesn't live as long, isn't the role model he wants to be for his family and dies filled with regrets and 'what ifs'

This example is no doubt going to the extreme, but it illustrates the point, as the decision you make right now can and will directly impact your future (especially if it's a regularly repeated action). Another way to think about this is the "butterfly effect". Do you know how in films when they go back in time and they worry about how one action can completely alter the future? Well, the "butterfly effect" is real, as every decision you make (even if it seems unimportant) can completely alter your trajectory.

That's why a huge part of thinking like a CEO is developing your ability to make decisions that take into consideration the long-term repercussions of your actions. Otherwise, every action based only on the first order of consequence will directly impact long-term growth, impact and sustainability.

This is also where the problem comes in, as often passing on first order consequences means making an in-the-moment sacrifice or tough decision with an immediately perceived pain. Like when you come across a customer who you know is going to be a nightmare. Turning down their business in the moment may sting, especially if you could have used the boost in cash flow. However, the headaches saved in the long run will far outweigh that in the moment discomfort. Yet this is exactly why so many people struggle with this, as they're so focused on what's in front of them, that they don't take the time to step back and view the ramifications of their actions. Or they don't have the mindset required to say no, even if it goes against their intuition or what others would do.

A perfect example of this is when a business is struggling and usually the first thing to be cut is spending in areas such as marketing or advertising. This may seem "safe" and a way to preserve cash, when in reality, it's just aggravating the situation long-term. After all, while that lifeline may save them for a couple of months, eventually, they'll be even worse off. Whereas even though investing in those areas during challenging times can seem terrifying, it's what is most likely to get them back on track and lead to growth. Meaning that panic-first order of consequence decision to save cash short-term, may very well be the reason why they go out of business.

That's why when you're faced with a decision, it's vital to look at the bigger picture and the future consequences, as even though it may feel uncomfortable, you may need to keep pushing or double down on a path of action. Is this easy? No, especially during times of escalated pressure. However, if you want to think like a CEO, then you simply can't afford to view problems or approach challenges with the same short-sighted mentality that others would.

I was in this spot a few months ago where we started focusing on scaling my business. Just to give you some context, the majority of my advertising is done through Facebook ads and while I know what I'm doing, I'm far from an expert. For that reason, I decided to invest $24k in the coaches and team I needed to help optimize my ads and scale what I'm doing to the next level. Now, most overwhelmed CEOs (myself included a few years ago) would have frozen at the amount. They'd be talking themselves out of it and justifying how it's too much money, so they'll just continue struggling on their own. Again, this goes back to that first order of consequence and focusing on the pain that comes with it (in cases like this, parting with cash). When you just focus on the first order, it will always seem like the wrong decision, as all you'll be thinking about is what you're giving up or have to lose. That's why instead when making big decisions it's vital to consider the potential gain or loss from staying stuck. In this situation, I focused on the bigger vision of where I wanted to get to and the positive ROI (along with speed) I could achieve with the right support. Which combined with the time I'd already lost and would continue to lose if I kept trying on my own, made it easy to trust my gut and follow through. Especially when I factored in how much potential growth and revenue was being lost for every day I didn't get this right.

Remember, as CEO, it's on you to think bigger, to make calculated decisions and to tie together short-term needs with the bigger vision of what you're striving towards. Obviously, that doesn't mean being reckless or throwing caution to the wind. Instead, it requires looking ahead and making decisions based on where you want to get to, not on where you are (I'll shortly be sharing with you a framework to do exactly that).

It's important to reiterate that the order of consequences applies to every area of your life. Whether it's skipping the gym, prioritizing working late over date night, procrastinating over that project, not picking up the phone to call that client, facing that difficult conversation, or any other action you know you need to take. Avoiding whatever you know you need to do often means you're giving in to the first order consequence, where you prioritize pleasure, comfort, or relief over the action you should (or shouldn't) be taking. In isolation this may seem inconsequential, but when added together the ramifications can be huge.

I remember an application call with a CEO I had a few years ago who had reached out to speak to me as he was stuck in a rut. As a recruitment firm, most of their business was generated from cold calling potential customers. Yet despite knowing that, he just couldn't bring himself to pick up the phone, an inaction that meant they hadn't closed a new client in weeks. Instead, he'd spend his days watching YouTube or engulfed in busy work, looking for any reason to avoid facing that potential rejection. The problem was, all of the setbacks had caused him to get stuck in his own head, where he was giving in to the first order of consequence and choosing comfort over potential pain. A cycle that had been going on for close to a year and that was costing him more than $25,000 a month.

He knew he couldn't carry on this way and that he needed help, but when it came down to moving forward with working together, he stalled. He came out with all sorts of excuses about how it wasn't the right time and he needed to preserve cash flow. In turn, focusing on and giving in to the first order of consequence, instead of taking the action that could get him out of his rut. This was a guy who, when we spoke, told me about his huge vision and passion, along with his desire to help other people secure the jobs of their dreams. For him, his greatest fear was having to give it all up and go back to working for someone else. Yet, after seeing one of his posts pop up on my LinkedIn feed recently, I saw that's exactly what had happened. He's closed down his business, let go of his team and is now back in a job, working for someone else. Now obviously I don't know the full story, so I'd never want to make assumptions. However, from my experience, I'd be shocked if it wasn't linked to him giving in to the first order of consequence by not picking up the phone or investing in help (whether it was with me or someone else).

The thing is though - when you turn that around and you make the tough call, that's how you take back control and put yourself in a position where your actions and decisions can change everything. One of my first-time tech CEO clients is a perfect example of exactly that. When we first spoke, his days were consumed by fires and never-ending demands. Which combined with trying to manage a growing team, bring in investment and generate revenue, was leaving him scattered, on a rollercoaster ride of emotions, anxious and overwhelmed. A state of mind that was causing him to second guess himself at every turn, avoid making decisions for weeks at a time, overthink everything he did and lose hours every day where he was unproductive or stuck in his own head. This cycle had been going on for months, leaving him burnt out, resenting his business and regularly facing periods where he felt trapped, as the sacrifices no longer felt like they were worth the reward.

Realizing he couldn't keep going on this way, he decided he needed to get help. Now, going through the same order of consequences, the first order was painful. Especially since at the time their runway was limited, they were struggling to secure more funding and he knew any expense that wasn't viewed as a "necessity" for the business would lead to a huge argument with his CFO (he tended to avoid these disagreements due to his difficulties in navigating them without getting emotional or defensive). On top of that, he also needed to swallow an element of pride, admitting he needed support, a barrier that many overwhelmed CEOs struggle to overcome.

Regardless, he trusted his gut and faced the first order of consequence by making a decision that he wanted us to work together. As a result, here are the next four consequences that came because of the actions he took – his domino effect if you'd like.

1) Once we audited what he was doing, he realized over 70% of his time was being spent on making other people happy, as he hadn't learned to let go, set the right boundaries, or say no. This realization was the push he needed to get clear on exactly what to focus on and prioritize, all while implementing the right systems to delegate, manage his time and free up the headspace to focus on tasks that grow the business.

2) By getting out of his own head, he was finally able to stop doubting himself and trust his own intuition, make timely decisions and step into the role of the CEO he needed to be to drive the business forward, inspire his team and steer them through the storm.

3) Because of his newfound clarity, confidence and conviction, he was able to secure more funding, close several major deals and take the business to new heights, positioning the company to create a greater impact on the world.

4) As a result, they've just had a huge evaluation, are leading the way in their industry and are on the brink of releasing technology that will change the world. On a personal level, as a CEO he's reignited that passion and spark, is no longer feeling burnt out, and to put it in his words, his business "no longer feels a big drain".

Now, most overwhelmed CEOs would have given in at that first consequence, saying "it's not the right time", "it's too much money" or making justifications of how they'll just do it on their own. Ironically wasting more time and money going round in circles, or due to the opportunity cost that comes with their inaction. Yet for this client, trusting his own gut for what he needed and making a short-term sacrifice that may have been uncomfortable upfront, paid off massively in the long run.

And this is exactly how successful CEOs make decisions. Take anyone from Elon Musk to Richard Branson or Bill Gates, and you'll see the pattern where rather than focusing on the short-term 'pain' or sacrifice, they look at the bigger picture taking actions that will influence the long-term vision. Now it's important to remember that throughout various stages of their careers, people have called them crazy, ridiculed their decisions or predicted they'd fail. Yet despite the backlash, they still persevered. Why? Because unlike the people criticizing them who were doing so based on viewing the first order of consequence, they knew the reason why they were taking certain actions, the vision they were trying to create and everything they had to gain. That's why they could trust their own convictions. Not only that, they also recognized the need to fail fast and adapt, as it is in those setbacks that you learn the biggest lessons and uncover the greatest opportunities for growth - a mentality and perspective on life that is exactly why they get and stay ahead.

So while "normal" people or those who are willing to settle for "average" can get away with focusing on in the moment decisions, if you want to be an effective CEO, then you have to think three steps ahead. That means looking at the bigger picture and fully understanding what you have to gain, factoring in all consequences and not rating them the same. Especially since consequence five is far more likely to have a greater payoff than consequence one. When you start to think this way or view decisions in this light, it will open you up to a whole new world of possibilities that before was limited only by your level of thinking.

What does this mean for you?

When we break it down, you can look at the choices you make on two levels: daily micro actions and bigger picture decisions. Both are important, yet they need to be handled in different ways.

Daily micro actions

These are the regular, reoccurring, small decisions you make daily which on their own may not have huge implications, but when compounded can have a snowball effect. Things like properly planning your day, getting in that workout, avoiding that conversation, missing date night etc. Dealing with these goes back to what we spoke about in section one, because at its core, this will come down to having the self-awareness of putting yourself at cause and taking responsibility for the decisions and actions that you take.

Whether it's in your business, getting that burger, skipping the gym, speaking to that person, cancelling dinner with your family or whatever else it may be, really stopping to ask yourself what is the bigger consequence of giving in to this first order? What else haven't you factored in? And what do you potentially lose (or gain) by taking or avoiding this action?

It sounds simple, but instead of just reacting or acting on impulse, stopping to take a moment to think through what you're facing and putting the situation into perspective may be exactly what you need to realign yourself with what you're doing and why. Doing so may also be the push you need to face that discomfort, stop procrastinating and take an action you know you need to take but have been avoiding.

The reason why I'm getting you to look at this from a holistic perspective is because it's vital to remember that you are more than just your role. Because of that, every part of your life is related, and it can and will directly affect the way you think, feel and behave.

For instance, one of my clients was having problems in his marriage, as he was working all the time and never at home. Meaning that when he was at work, he felt guilty for not being with his family, yet when he was at home, he felt guilty for not working. An inner conflict which was hugely detrimental to the business's growth, as he was never fully present or focused on what he was doing. Another client was burning the candle at both ends to the point she was living on take out, never exercising and neglecting sleep. Leaving her burnt out and exhausted. In both of these cases, their actions outside their role directly impacted their performance in their role, as it influenced everything from their focus to their energy, how they showed up, their productivity and how they inspired others.

That's why if you want to perform at the highest level, it's vital you have all these other areas in check. Doing so means holding yourself to a higher standard and making the tough choices, even when they're inconvenient, challenging, or you simply don't want to.

Before going any further, I want to challenge you to stop for a moment and think about a first order of consequence you gave into this week. Maybe you delayed facing that conversation, spent time scrolling through the newsfeed instead of starting that report, made an excuse to your partner about why you needed to work late, or you sat on the couch watching Netflix instead of hitting the gym.

Got one?

With that in mind – what are the consequences of that action? Especially if you continue repeating it long-term? Maybe it'll lead to less revenue, a toxic member remaining in your team, your health continuing to deteriorate, or a breakdown in your relationship?

On the flip side, what do you have to gain if you follow through with this the next time you face this decision? And how can you remind and push yourself to ensure that you do?

As mentioned before, sometimes just putting these decisions into perspective is exactly what you need to break through that mental block. Going back to section one though – remember that reflecting on this is never about blame, as all that will do is cause a negative state of beating yourself up or dwelling on the past. Instead, it's about bringing the moment into your awareness, learning from your actions and deciding how to better handle the same situation in the future.

Because of that, a good rule to live by is whenever you're faced with such decisions, always push yourself towards facing the 'painful' consequence of the first order. Yes, it may not feel great and in the moment, you may even resent doing so, but the reality is that while the fuzzy feel-good emotions may come along with the first order, the other ramifications of your actions could have huge consequences (not always, but I'm sure you get the picture). Once again, your in the moment decision (which in isolation may seem irrelevant), can and will directly influence your future. Especially when you add them together.

When you start approaching life and the choices you make in this way, the entire game will change. As a result, you'll create a huge momentum shift in your thoughts, actions and decisions, which ultimately will directly affect your income, impact and freedom.

Understanding the bigger picture

Whether it's in your life or business, when it comes to making huge decisions, it's vital you look at what's happening from every angle to ensure that nothing is missed or overlooked. By ensuring you have all the details and you've factored in every scenario, it will make it easier to follow through with even the toughest choices. To help you do exactly that, I want to share with you a decision-making framework I use with clients whenever we need to dissect a decision and determine a course of action.

The reason why this framework works, is it takes you through four questions that will help you gain holistic clarity on the situation you're facing. To get the most out of this, grab a pen and paper and write the answers down. By doing so, you'll be able to get all the ideas out of your head, making it easier for you to consciously step back, process what's in front of you and then decide what action to take.

Start by putting the decision you're trying to make at the top of the page, then break the page into four segments. From there go through them one at a time and ask yourself:

Firstly: if you take this action, what will happen?

Secondly: if you take this action, what won't happen?

Thirdly: if you don't take this action, what will happen?

And finally: if you don't take this action, what won't happen?

By using these four questions you'll be able to look at the decision from every angle, ensuring you factor in all the key points, potential outcomes and consequences of the action you take.

Once you've put everything down and you've processed what the options are, you can then stop and ask yourself "knowing everything I now know, what is the best path going forward?"

One big thing to add is that when it comes to huge decisions, we all tend to get in a tunnel vision of what's happening and we're unable to see the other, more long-term factors surrounding the situation. Or, despite knowing what we need to do, we get attached to the outcomes or focus on the wrong variables. As we spoke about before, if you want to be a highly effective CEO, then it's vital that you never make decisions based on emotion or fear. Instead, ensure you consider the full picture of risks, rewards, short-term sacrifices, and long-term gains. For that reason, when it comes to making key decisions, you may want to consider getting an outside counsel who is completely detached from your business. Find someone you trust, who can bring in different perspectives and ask the right questions to ensure you haven't missed anything. On the flip side of that – also audit your own intuition and ensure you're not falling into the trap of looking for someone to make the decision for you, or talk you out of actions you know you need to take. After all, you're CEO for a reason and while it helps to have someone who can help you not overlook anything, at the end of the day you know the vision, business and reasons better than anyone, which is ultimately why the decision rests with you.

Regardless of the clarity you gain with this tool, I know that at times huge decisions can be terrifying, especially when they're based on bigger picture growth that requires short-term sacrifices. That's why it's so important to remember that you are never going to know the alternative to any decision you make. So while it's easy to overthink or worry about "what if" you go down the wrong path, the reality is you will never know for certain. Not only that, but at times despite your best intentions, things can and will go wrong, and chances are you'll always have to adjust and factor in new variables along the way.

If you look at some of the greatest CEOs of our time, you'll often hear them talk about the need to fail fast. That's because you will often need to take action and make mistakes to figure out the correct path and approach. This is why instead of pressuring yourself to be "perfect", it's always better to take decisive action than to stall and stay stuck. After all, even if you do make a mistake, you can always correct your course or pivot. Because of that, the sooner you take the unnecessary pressure off yourself, the sooner you'll be able to create momentum and move forward. Again, that doesn't mean being reckless, but it does mean at times taking calculated risks when they're in alignment with the outcome you're aiming to create.

In many ways, doing this confidently and effectively will come down to knowing your goals, as that will be a huge factor in deciding whether or not an action is the correct decision.

Knowing your goals

When it comes to goal setting and execution, I find that for most overwhelmed CEOs, one of three scenarios tends to happen:

1) They sit down once a year, set some targets because they feel like it's something they "should do", then they dive straight back into the trenches, rarely looking back at them.
2) They get so caught up in their big vision and where they want to be in five years, that they don't know where to begin with setting goals or targets.
3) Despite knowing their goals, they get so pulled into firefighting and daily problems, that they don't get the time to drive them forward.

The reality is that none of these approaches are ever going to lead to any real level of growth or impact. If you want to think and make decisions like an Evolved CEO, it's vital you keep these goals top of mind, using them to guide you in everything that you do.

That's why I'm not a big fan of 12-month goals. Sure, it's great to have an idea of where you want to be a year from now. But the problem is that 12 months is a long time. Meaning life could change, what you're doing could be turned upside down and due to the duration, there are variables that simply can't be accounted for. Now don't get me wrong, setting 12-month goals is still important, but if you want to be highly intentional with what you do, then I believe you need to take it a step further and break those goals down into 90-day targets. These targets can then become tangible because you can set real outcomes and objectives. Not only that, but it also becomes far easier to measure and adapt along the way.

The way I recommend thinking about goal setting is to:

1) Get clear on where you want to be 12 months from now.
2) Reverse engineer the journey, figuring out where you'd need to be in 90 days to be on track for your 12 months goal to be achieved.
3) Break that down into your focus for the next seven days.
4) Every week assess progress, reflect on key lessons and set actions for the next seven days, in accordance with what needs to happen to further your 90-day objectives.
5) Repeat and adapt, pivoting, adjusting, or realigning wherever necessary.
6) Then every quarter reassess the next 90-day goals and set new objectives.

This works because it allows you to take your macro vision and break it down into micro focuses. Meaning that every week you know exactly what you need to focus on to move towards your goals. This is how you ensure that you keep momentum, and it also enables you to stay laser-focused, while tracking progress and ensuring you're on target.

By thinking this way, you'll also be able to get out of the cycle of just allowing your days to be spent on short-term problems. Instead, you'll be able to tie your planning to the bigger picture of what you want to achieve. Ensuring you can find the right balance between long-term thinking and short-term priorities.

One of my first-time CEO clients was the prime example of someone who got stuck in the short-term trap. When we first met, as the CEO of a growing tech company, his primary focus was to bring in investment and funding. On top of that, he also needed to manage an expanding team, overlook operations, deal with stakeholders and a whole host of other responsibilities.

To keep on top of his days he'd follow the standard productivity practice of creating a to-do list and tackling the most important tasks for the day first. On paper, this sounds like great advice, as why wouldn't you do the most important task first? But in reality, following practices like this can be catastrophic for CEOs, especially when it comes to long-term growth. After all, lists like these are often short-sighted, keeping you focused on short-term problems over bigger picture priorities.

In this client's case, as his main focus was securing funding, it meant that the bulk of his time needed to be spent on pitches, writing and creating presentations. However, by creating a to-do list of the day's top priorities, it meant he was focusing on tasks that felt important for that day, and not factoring in the bigger picture of what needed to get done. As a result, his days would get consumed by short-term reactionary problems, meaning that if he was lucky, he'd maybe get an hour at the end of the day to focus on high-value work. This caused a huge amount of frustration, as not only were these high-value tasks not getting the attention they needed, but by the time he got to them, he was mentally drained and exhausted. Causing him to be nowhere near the high energy state of flow he needed to be in to effectively execute on these tasks. So they either didn't get done at all, weren't done to a high standard, or the progress was so slow that it didn't matter anyway.

That's why your planning needs to be tied to the bigger picture, because as a CEO, you simply can't afford to allow short-term problems to consume the bulk of your day. Especially since if the client mentioned didn't secure further investment, there wouldn't be a company with fires to get pulled into anyway. Because of that, we needed to reorganize his schedule. We identified his best energy flow was in the morning, so we blocked off his calendar, between 9 and 12 each day. This is the time he would only use for high-value work and only after lunch did he get into the day-to-day responsibilities. A shift that put him back in control of his time and meant he could prioritize tasks that actually pushed the business forward, all while ensuring he didn't drop the ball on other responsibilities either. Again, this goes back to thinking like a CEO and recognizing where your time has the greatest impact and ensuring it takes priority. To take it a step further, we also implemented a rule that he wouldn't check his email in the morning either. The reason being is it's far too easy for a problem to enter your inbox and take over your focus, where even though you tell yourself you'll sort it later, you can't stop thinking about what needs to get done. Because of that, he needed to protect his attention, ensuring that his bandwidth was free and focused on the task at hand.

Now, I don't want us to get off course, which is why I'm not going to go through how to do all this, as it's literally the entire first section of my book *"The Effective CEO"*. But in short, what you need to do is figure out your zone of genius – as in what tasks and work can only be done by you, along with your high-value growth tasks and long-term targets - then schedule that first. That's the real secret to ensuring you can prioritize time for tasks that create growth and further your vision.

Auditing new ideas

Every day as CEO you'll probably be presented with new ideas, paths and opportunities. Yet, in reality, you're never going to be able to pursue them all, which is why at times you'll have to make a tough call or decision on what to focus on and give your attention to. This however is where overwhelmed CEOs become their own worst enemy. They get caught up bouncing around from one thing to the next, taking on more than they can handle and stretching themselves thin. Evolved CEOs however recognize that time is their most valuable resource, which is why when it comes to thinking like a CEO, one of the biggest realizations to make is that what you don't do, is just as important as what you do do.

I saw this a few months ago on a call with one of my clients, who started the session all excited about a new venture he'd been presented with. And it sounded great, but the issue was that for the last few months they had put everything into an upcoming launch and because of it he was already short on time. So even though this new opportunity sounded great, diverting his focus could massively damage the launch and hard work the team had put in. Meaning that in the bigger picture, saying no (for now anyway) was a far better path of action.

This is why to think like a CEO, it's vital you know your goals, vision and objectives and use that to guide you in your decisions. Doing so will go a long way in helping you avoid shiny object syndrome and ensure you stay focused and on course. Again, this goes back to the order of consequences and at times it will mean making short-term sacrifices to not lose sight of bigger picture targets.

The way I always encourage my private clients to think about this is whenever you're presented with a new opportunity, ask yourself: does this tie into your 90-day targets? If the answer is no, then is this going to get you closer to your goals? If the answer is still no, then is this really going to be the best use of your time, or is it going to take you away from what you need to do?

By going through this questioning, you can audit what you decide to take on. One thing you can do as well is to create what I call an *"idea bank"*. Essentially, you take all these opportunities and place them in a spreadsheet along with all the thoughts and ideas you have for them. That way you can get them out of your head and consciously disconnect from the idea without the fear that you'll forget key details. Then every quarter when you're setting new targets you can go back to the *"idea bank"* and see what ties into your vision and what opportunities you want to pursue.

Again, this is all broken down in my book *"The Effective CEO"*, but regardless I wanted to include an overview, as understanding these concepts will be a huge factor in your focus and decision making – especially when it comes to long-term thinking.

If you want to dive into this further, grab a copy of *"The Effective CEO"* at: **https://byronmorrison.com/theeffectiveceo**

Staying on course

When it comes to longevity as a CEO, one of your defining factors will be your ability to weather the storms and handle the ups and downs that come with running and growing a business. The truth is it's not easy, and there will probably be numerous times you'll be pushed to your limit. For one of my clients, this was a reoccurring challenge. In the six years that he'd been growing his start-up, he'd have several instances a year where the setbacks in gaining funding, building traction and bringing their product to market would cause him to spiral into a pit of anxiety, self-doubt and stress. When we got to the root cause of why this happened, we uncovered that it stemmed off his frustration over the business not being further along than he thought they'd be. Whenever this happened, he'd become deflated, feeling like he wanted to throw in the towel and burn the business down. Not only was this a huge drain on him mentally and emotionally, it also meant that whenever he was in this state, he was unproductive, making emotional decisions and simply going through the motions, stifling growth.

In our time together, I found that this happened whenever he lost sight of the vision of "why" he started the business in the first place. Instead of focusing on a higher purpose or greater good, his bandwidth would be consumed by fires and daily challenges. It was no wonder he'd often lose his passion. When every day feels like you just went 12 rounds with Mike Tyson, the thought of surviving can quickly get in the way of remembering why you got in the ring in the first place.

Because of that, anytime he started feeling this way, the immediate action I'd get him to take was to disconnect and take some time to sit down, revisit his goals and realign himself with what he was doing. Not just in business, but on a personal level as well. This simple action in itself was often exactly what he needed to reignite that fire, refocus and keep pushing during challenging times.

When you've been pushed to your limit, feel unfocused or like giving up, reconnecting with why you went down that road in the first place or where you're trying to get to may be exactly what you need to regain motivation and momentum. That's why as part of the mental preparation process I get my clients to go through every morning, I encourage them to go over their goals. This doesn't need to take long, but by doing so they can start their day focused on what they want to achieve and can ensure the actions they take are aligned with the bigger picture outcomes they want to create.

As for the full mental preparation morning process, it's unfortunately beyond the scope of this book. The reason being is there are various exercises I need to take you through to help you gain clarity on who is that next level, evolved version of yourself. Just to give you an idea though, once we have that clarity, that's when we can reverse engineer the journey, uncovering the habits, beliefs, routines, and non-negotiable parts of their day that you need to take on to evolve into that more confident, more engaged, more powerful, next level version of yourself. We can then turn that clarity into a morning ritual to get you into the right state of mind and embody that new identity, so that you can show up as the best version of yourself each and every day. I do however break this entire process down in my Unshakeable course as well.

Final thoughts

When it comes to big picture thinking, it's vital to remember that momentum is not linear. Meaning that at times you can have huge growth, everything is flowing and seems to be working, whereas at other times despite doing everything right, you can become stagnant.

That's why I always warn my clients to prepare themselves for this to happen, because even when you feel on top of the world, you need to remember it's not a matter of "if" it stalls, it's a matter of "when". By being aware of this, you can mentally prepare yourself for how to handle these periods, as rather than being reactive, you can proactively act in a way that helps you regain traction.

It's important to note that often when things are going well, this is when people tend to feel invincible and like they can do more. As a result, they often let their habits slip, along with the behaviours and routines that were the foundation of why they felt good in the first place. That's why in times you feel off, less focused or not as energized as usual, it's vital to take a step back and really ask yourself what are you neglecting? As it may be a case that you need to cut down on long hours, get back on track with your eating, or even go to bed on time. Remember, it is often these outside factors that have the biggest impact on your ability to show up effectively as a CEO.

When looking ahead at the bigger picture and what's on the horizon, you can factor in periods of disruption. For instance, with one of my clients, every few months he'd have a period of three weeks where he'd be doing longer hours, more high bandwidth tasks, have extensive meetings and be under extra pressure. A cycle that by the end, would leave him exhausted. When we broke down what was happening, I uncovered that during these periods he was sacrificing sleep, barely exercised and really wasn't looking after himself, all to free up time to focus on work. When in reality, it was during these periods he actually needed to double down on these actions. With that in mind, he agreed to make it non-negotiable to revisit his goals daily, meditate, work out (even if it was a short burst at home if he didn't have time for the gym), have healthy meals prepared and protect his sleep hygiene. By making this shift, he's now getting through these periods energized, consistently performing throughout and able to bring his A-game when it matters most.

Again, this comes down to thinking like a CEO – where instead of allowing yourself to get caught up in the moment or derailed by everyday problems, you look ahead, having clarity on where you're going, what you're doing and to the best of your ability, following through with what you can control.

Strategic thinking task

This section has been all about helping you think bigger, make better decisions and balance short-term priorities with your long-term vision. That clarity however is only one piece of the puzzle, which is why I've got a task to help you take it to the next level.

Here's what I want you to do:

1) Take some time to reflect on where you want to be 90-days from now. Not just in your business, but in every area of your life.

Think about what's your vision? What are your biggest goals? What does the life you want to live look like?

The key thing here is to set tangible objectives, as if you just say, "I want more money", that doesn't mean anything. After all, technically a dollar is more. That's why instead, you need to be specific, getting clear on what you actually want and tying it to either a tangible number, or an event.

You're not going to be able to hit a target you don't know, so you need to get really specific with what you want.

Maybe you want to hit a revenue target, launch a new venture by a certain date, or take 'x' number of hours off each week.

Once you know what you want, the next step is to think about:

2) Who do you need to become to make this happen? What are the habits, routines, rituals and non-negotiables you need to take on to turn this into a reality?

This part is key, as when it comes to goals, many people talk a big game, telling everyone how they're going to become the next Elon Musk or make a billion dollars. Yet when it comes down to it, their actions simply do not match their ambitions.

Because of that, if you want to master the mindset needed to crush your goals and breakthrough to the next level, then you need to realize that it is you who needs to evolve. Think of it like this – you are what you repeatedly do, which is why what made you who you are today, isn't going to help you become who you want to be tomorrow. If anything, your current habits, behaviours and routines are actually what is holding you back.

That's why I want you to take some time and think about who do you need to become?

Who do you need to become to create more impact? To double, triple or quadruple your income? To effectively lead, inspire others and create a life of freedom on your terms?

And with that in mind, how do you need to show up to take control of the life that you want?

Remember - if you want to think like that next level CEO, then you can't make decisions as the old version of yourself. Because if you do, nothing is going to change and you will stay where you are. Instead, you need to make decisions as the future version of yourself. As that version of you who is making millions of dollars. Who is impacting millions of lives. Who is changing the world. Whatever your goal is, you need to think, act and behave as the version of yourself who made that vision a reality. That in turn will tie back into the order of consequences, where you take actions and make decisions based on where you want to get to, not on where you are.

Share your thoughts

I'd love to hear your thoughts on what we've discussed so far. Join the community and share your questions, biggest takeaways, or your own insights that you'd add to what was discussed in this book. After all, your unique perspective could go a long way in challenging another CEO's status quo, or enabling them to see ways of dealing with the challenges they're facing.

Also feel free to share your tasks and reflections, as in doing so I can provide feedback for you in the group, you can learn from others, and it can also be a way to keep yourself accountable so that you can ensure you follow through.

You can access the community at:

https://www.facebook.com/groups/impactdrivenceos

Section 3

Get out of your own head

If you want to consistently perform at the level needed to be a highly effective CEO, then one skill you have to master is getting out of your own head. Now, this is easier said than done, which is why most overwhelmed CEOs tend to allow the doubts, fears and sabotaging thoughts stop them from showing up at their best or taking the actions they should be taking.

The problem is that when something goes wrong, you face a challenge or get put in an uncomfortable position, the usual response is to mentally go straight to a story. Where subconsciously, you start convincing yourself of an outcome or how a situation will play out before it even happens.

These stories can be present for various reasons, from being at the effect of the past to focusing on the wrong things, or going back to what we spoke about in section one - because your brain is programmed for survival. Regardless of the reason, this will likely explain why at times you procrastinate, overthink, second-guess yourself, or fear that you'll fail.

It's important to remember that this happens in every area of our lives. A few examples I've seen recently in conversations is people avoiding putting videos on social media due to a fear that they'll get judged. Fearing picking up the phone because they worry they'll be rejected. Losing a potential client and immediately thinking it's because they're not good enough. Feeling like an imposter who will get ousted as a fraud after achieving a new level of success. Or even avoiding attending a fitness class due to fearing they won't be as good as everyone else and will get laughed at.

The stories you tell yourself may be similar, or they could be completely different. Regardless, it's important to remember that in none of these situations do you have any certainty that will be the outcome. Yet subconsciously, your focus hones in on the perceived worst-case scenario, where you're convinced that will happen, even though there is no possible way for you to know. To make matters worse, by focusing on the worst-case scenario, you overhype the situation, somehow convincing yourself it's the end of the world, when in reality, even if it does come true, in most cases it probably isn't that big a deal. Yet allowing that story to consume you can have an almost paralysing effect, especially when it takes over your energy and bandwidth.

One of my CEO clients used to do this all of the time. I remember one conversation during a period when they were fundraising. That week they'd had a pretty big setback in their pilot program, they had been passed over for a government grant and were going through the usual "everything is falling apart" cycle founders tend to find themselves in every few weeks.

This client then received an email from their biggest investor saying he wanted a sit-down meeting with him and the other two founders. This is something he had never requested before, which is why it caused a huge amount of panic in him. The story he immediately jumped to was that this meeting was because the investor wanted to drop them and wouldn't be in for their next round of funding. A fear that, understandably, was causing a huge amount of anxiety and overwhelm.

As I said before, this client tended to allow these stories to get him stuck in his own head, especially since they were always focused on worst-case scenarios. What I needed to do was to get him to realign his focus, mentally take a step back and ask himself – does he know this for certain? Or is this just a story he's telling himself?

Because here's the thing – if you want to think like a CEO, you simply can't afford to allow these stories to cause you to get stuck in your own head. Because that's when you take actions or make decisions based on emotion or fear, which is always going to be short-sighted. Especially since when you jump to a story, your actions, thoughts and behaviours tend to come into alignment, where it then becomes a self-fulfilling prophecy, and you sabotage your success. Reaffirming to yourself that story was right. Like if you've ever been anxious about doing a presentation, so mentally you jump to a story about how you'll mumble your words or won't perform properly. Because of that, all that anxious energy builds up inside you as you're focused on how you'll mess up. Meaning that of course you won't show up at your best.

That's why for this client whenever this happened and he realized it was just a story, we could start to reframe it, figuring out what else could be happening instead? What other paths could play out? Is it really likely to be as bad as the story in his head?

In the end, despite the setbacks, the investor wanted to sit down with the team as he truly believed in their vision and what they were doing, so he wanted to know how else he could help. Especially since he had some other connections he could introduce them to and wanted to see how else he could support them in gaining more traction. Meaning this meeting he had been building up in his head as being this huge catastrophe, was actually a positive.

One of my favourite sayings is "if you stress about something before it happens, you put yourself through it twice". And that's exactly what happens when you allow yourself to jump to a story and preconceived outcome. Getting this right definitely isn't easy, especially since this reaction is linked to our subconscious programming. But if you want to think like a CEO, you have to catch yourself in the act, figure out why you're jumping to a story, why you're being at effect and what action you need to take to get it under control.

Because if you allow yourself to get stuck in that story – then it's game over.

Another example is a client who during a hiring phase found an incredible candidate. She was exactly who he thought the team needed and he was so excited about her potentially coming on board. Yet unfortunately, she turned down their offer. We got on a call and he felt completely deflated, convinced the reason why she declined to join the team was because of him. He took the rejection to heart, viewing it as a reflection of himself and that he wasn't good enough. In that moment I challenged him to think – did he know this for certain? Or was it just a story he was telling himself? After we broke it down, he started to feel better, as he realized that he was so focused on his perception of the outcome, that he hadn't stopped to process the other variables that could have influenced her decision. In the end, he got on another call with her and she reiterated that she loved the company and the vision. The problem though was that as a start-up they were limited in what they could pay her. Whereas a bigger company had just offered her a position for three times the salary. Not only that, but for this stage in her career and with a young family, she wanted stability and calmness, not the rollercoaster of stress and chaos that comes with life in a start-up. Therefore, despite her wishing she could accept the role, she had to take the other offer, as it was ultimately better for her and her family. One thing she re-emphasized though was that she would love to be involved with them in the future, and if there was any other way she could help them she would. That's how deeply she connected with their mission and the impact they were trying to make.

This is a perfect example of how easy it is to get stuck in your own head. Where something happens and you jump straight to some made-up story that has nothing to do with the actual situation. A reaction that for this client, caused a whole host of inner turmoil and self-doubt.

Because of that, whenever you find yourself focusing on the future or a perceived problem that hasn't happened yet, stop, take a deep breath, and ask yourself – do I know this for certain? Or is this just a story I'm telling myself? And if it's just a story, think about how else it could play out, along with how you need to put yourself at cause and focus on the actions you need to take.

With that being said though, chances are this won't magically solve the problem or remove all the negative feelings that come with the situation. But it can go a long way in putting your thoughts and feelings into perspective. Doing so will also enable you to process what is really going on and determine the best path of action going forward. Remember: you are never going to be in complete control of what's going on around you, but the one thing you can always control is how you choose to respond to it. So question every story, allow yourself time to process situations and ensure you make decisions based on reality and not perceptions. Once you start doing that, you'll unlock a whole new level of confidence, clarity and conviction that will allow you to view the world in a completely different light.

I know I said this before, but I'll keep repeating this until it sinks in. In times of challenges and frustrations, it's only a bad thing if you keep repeating the same problematic actions in the future. Whereas despite the discomfort, it is in these setbacks that you have the greatest opportunity to learn and grow. Because of that, ensure you always stop to reflect on what happened, what you need to take away from the situation and how you can improve for the future. That's how you evolve and take control.

Why we get anxious

Before one of my clients and I met, he'd had a pretty tough year in business. They'd lost several clients, he had to let go of members of his team and business was struggling. As I'm sure you can imagine, this was an incredibly stressful time, and it understandably was placing a huge strain on him mentally. When we started looking at what was happening, I found out that the way he built his business was through networking events. It made sense, he's a people person, is able to forge great relationships and it's where his target market spends their time. Yet for the last few months, the thought alone of attending these events was spiking his anxiety to the point he was frozen in fear, where at times he felt so overwhelmed, he was unable to leave the house. Leaving him feeling trapped, as he just couldn't bring himself to face the one action that could get the business back on track.

As we dived in further, it became clear that this was happening because the story he was telling himself was keeping him stuck in his own head. As business hadn't been going well, he had convinced himself that everyone in that room would judge him, thinking he was a fraud and talk behind his back about how he was a failure. A belief that was making him so anxious he'd completely break out in sweat. This in turn would make the situation even worse, as it amplified his fear that people would stare, wondering what was wrong with him. So even though he knew what he needed to do, this mental block had him frozen in place, and he just couldn't bring himself to face these events.

It's important to understand that when you get anxious, it's for two reasons:

1) Viewing a future event in a negative light.
2) Not believing you can handle it properly.

Whether it's speaking to that person, delivering that presentation, attending that fitness class or whatever else you want to do – the reason why you get anxious is because the story you're telling yourself is focused on how bad it's going to go, along with how you'll mess it up, won't be able to do it, or you'll be unable to handle the situation.

That's exactly what was happening to this client, as he had convinced himself that upon walking into that room of judgment, he'd crumble and fall apart.

Dealing with anxiety

When you find yourself getting anxious, you need to interrupt those patterns by stopping, taking big deep breaths (again to lower your blood pressure and regain your ability to think clearly), then stop and ask yourself:

What are you anxious about?

What SPECIFICALLY is causing you anxiety?

The "*specifically*" part is key, because you need to be aware of what is actually going on and causing you to feel that way. Because once you know, then you need to shift it.

Instead of focusing on everything that could go wrong, ask yourself what could go right?

What happens when you get amazing results? You follow through and succeed?

Or even if it doesn't, is it really the end of the world like you're building up to be in your head?

You can see from this how it relates back to cause and effect, and why it's so important to master the ability to stop, become aware of what's happening and put yourself at cause for the actions you take. Especially since most of the time, the story you tell yourself is based on some worst-case scenario that is highly unlikely to ever happen.

Going back to that client who was avoiding networking events, we dissected the problem further and he came to terms with the fact that this was just a story. The reality was, no one in that room knew his business or what was going on behind closed doors. Meaning there was no possible way that story could be true. Upon realizing that, he agreed to face his fear and later that week he attended a networking event. Now, as this fear had been crippling him for so long, it didn't suddenly go away. He still felt anxious. However, he had reduced that anxiety to a level in which he could face what he needed to do. Regardless, upon arriving at the event, I encouraged him to go to the restroom, lock himself in a stall, close his eyes and breathe, calming himself down by putting the situation into perspective and going through the questions I shared with you above. Once he felt grounded, he then mentally imagined how he was going to walk into that room. He visualized how he was going to show up as the best, most powerful version of himself. How he was going to engage with others, speak with confidence and take control of that fear.

The result? He crushed it. He made some amazing new connections and such a good impression that they invited him back the following week to do a presentation. This scenario was far away from the story he'd been telling himself about how this would turn out. Fast forward 12 months and he is actually running his own networking event. He made a complete turnaround from someone who at one point was allowing the fear of judgement and story he was telling himself to prevent him from leaving the house.

Here's the key thing to remember: you are not the story in your head.

That's why it's so important to question every story and challenge every fear. Always stop to ask yourself "do I know this for certain, or is it just a story I'm telling myself?". And if it's just a story, how else could it turn out? What action do you need to take? As sometimes just putting the challenge or situation into perspective and refocusing on the true picture is exactly what you need to take control.

Getting out of your own head is going to be one of the defining skillsets needed to be able to think and perform at the level needed to be an effective CEO. This and this alone could be the difference between whether you become the bottleneck, or lead those around you to huge levels of impact and success.

With that being said though, it's simply unrealistic to put pressure on yourself to think you'll be immune to getting stuck in stories, stress and overwhelm. Or that you won't have to deal with the negative emotions that come with them. At the end of the day, regardless of how much deep work or personal development you do, you are only human. And that's ok. What truly matters is your ability to become aware of what's happening, how it's affecting you and navigating those challenges as your best self. The more you do that, the more confidence you'll create, as you'll start to see and believe that regardless of the challenge in front of you, that you can handle it and get through.

Speaking of getting stuck in your own head, the next block to deal with is overwhelm.

The truth about overwhelm

Between all the fires, never-ending challenges, huge pressure and made-up stories, the reality is that running a business and being a CEO can be pretty overwhelming. In fact, this is one of the biggest challenges clients come to me for help with. I saw this in a conversation with a new client, where before signing up, he told me about how he was tired of feeling overwhelmed by everything going on around him. He felt like he was spending 70% of his time in an overwhelmed state and he'd regularly have days where it would reach 4pm and he'd look back with no clue what he did or where his time went. It was so frustrating for him, as he wanted to be focused and clear-headed. Yet instead, he felt trapped in a cloudy mental chaos, unsure what to focus on or prioritize and on a rollercoaster ride of ups and downs. A pressure made even worse by the fact that as he had a growing team and clients depending on him, fuelling his biggest fear of letting down his employees, his family and himself.

Here's the thing though...

In most cases when someone tells me they're OVERwhelmed, they're actually... UNDERplanned. And it's because of all those scattered thoughts, competing agendas and stresses racing through their head, that they end up in an overwhelmed state.

To make matters worse, I find that often when people get overwhelmed, they tend to frantically rush around, trying to cram more in or push through, oblivious to how detrimental these actions are. I saw this with a new client who told me that as soon as she woke up, all she could think about was what she needed to get done. So she'd grab a coffee and within a few minutes of being awake she'd be at her desk starting work. In her mind, she had so much to do that every minute counted. Leading her to justify that she simply didn't have time to plan her days or figure out what she needed to do. Instead, she opted to just deal with the first fire that hit her inbox or problem that was top of mind.

From the outside, it's easy to see what the problem is. Or a huge part of it, anyway. Approaching her day in this way meant she was constantly in a reactive state, forever dealing with the next unknown problem and never getting a chance to give time to truly drive the company forward. The thing is, she isn't alone, and I speak to so many overwhelmed CEOs who act exactly the same way.

Which is why the irony in her being oblivious to her actions is not her fault. It can easily happen when you're under so much pressure and time constraints, that it feels like the last thing you can do is stop or slow down. That, however, is usually the time in which you need to do it the most. Especially since when you're in a state of response, stressed and mentally scattered, there's no way you can make the right decisions, think clearly, or perform at your best. Even though it may go against all your instincts, the best path of action may be to step away, recalibrate and allow yourself to get clear on what needs to be done. Luckily, there is a process to do exactly that.

How to deal with overwhelm

I've found the easiest way to deal with overwhelm is actually the simplest. Pretend for a moment it's 1995, grab a pen and paper, disconnect from your devices, and find somewhere quiet. Then without overthinking, do a brain dump and write down everything that is causing you to feel overwhelmed. It can be anything, like a project you're working on, a conversation you need to have, a task you haven't started yet, fire you need to put out, car insurance you need to sort out. Whatever is racing through your mind personally and professionally, get all of it down and in front of you.

By writing all this down, you'll be able to consciously disconnect from the thoughts in your head, and once they're in front of you, it'll be far easier to detach and process what's going on. After all, when all of those scattered thoughts are racing through your mind, it can be difficult to make sense of what's happening. But once you've got them in front of you, then you can go through them point by point and ask yourself – what do I need to do for this? What action do I need to take? What is the first step?

The reason why this is so important is that often you get overwhelmed because you mentally jump to the end result, worrying about everything that needs to get completed, what you haven't done, or that could go wrong along the way. Again, spinning up a story that causes you to get stuck in your own head. Which understandably, causes you to feel overwhelmed. To make matters worse, when you have so many competing thoughts and agendas going through your head, they can quickly get scrambled. Causing you to bounce around from one thought to the next, unable to make sense of what's happening or act on any of them.

When you stop and break it down though, it becomes more manageable, as you can figure out the first steps and actions you need to take. From there, you can then formulate a game plan and it becomes far less overwhelming when you know what you need to do.

As part of my Evolved program where I help CEOs take control of their role, beyond our weekly implementation calls, one feature I have is what I call "SOS" calls. Essentially these are calls for clients who need immediate support for when something happens that can't wait till our next session. The reason why I include them is I'd much rather sort a challenge straight away, instead of allowing it to manifest or spiral out of control. In the past these calls have been used for everything from calming nerves and anxiety before a big presentation, recalibrating before a board meeting, or discussing how to deal with a problematic employee before having a difficult conversation. I find however that most often, they're needed when a client is feeling overwhelmed.

An SOS call I had a few days ago is a perfect example. When we got on the phone, the client was feeling incredibly stressed, as he had so many things to get done (both personally and business-wise) that he just didn't know where to begin. Because of that, he'd just spent the last three hours mentally shut down, frozen in analysis paralysis and mindlessly watching YouTube instead of doing any work. An action that caused even more stress and overwhelm from how much he was beating himself up over wasting time. Like I said before, he was feeling overwhelmed because all those thoughts were racing through his head, and he hadn't stopped or taken the time to really figure out what he needed to do.

I took him through the brain dump exercise I just shared with you, taking all of his racing thoughts and compiling a list of what needed to get done. This included everything from completing some website copy, approving a new hire ad, sorting an issue with his accountant, booking an appointment with his dentist, speaking to his CFO and a few other challenges. By listing them down, we got them out of his head. From there, we went through them one by one, figuring out what action he needed to take. By the end, he was calm, everything felt manageable, and he knew exactly what he needed to do. He also realized that many of these issues weren't that big a deal and they could be solved in a few minutes or handed over to a member of his team, helping him feel back in control.

Going back to what I said before though, because he convinced himself he was far too busy, he hadn't stopped to process and figure out what needed to get done or how to do it. And as a result, the 15 minutes he told himself he didn't have, ended up losing him several hours in unfocused and unproductive time. Not to mention the huge amount of unnecessary stress and aggravation that came with it.

The reason why this practice is so powerful, is because it forces you to stop in your tracks, to take a step back and really understand what's going on. From there you can then determine the best path forward and how to handle it. The clarity may even reveal that you need to make some serious changes in how you spend your time – especially if once you know what you need to do, there's still no feasible way to get it done.

I saw this with another client whose list was so big and intensive, that even if there were three of him, he still wouldn't get it all done. The problem for him was he was allowing himself to spend too much time and energy on tasks he shouldn't even be involved in.

But because he hadn't taken the time to audit what he had on his plate, he simply acted on those tasks on autopilot. Realizing the errors in his ways, the logical step was to hire a VA to take over some day-to-day admin, manage his inbox and either flag important emails or respond to simple queries. He also determined that too much time was being spent on social media posting content and responding to messages. Meaning he needed a social media manager to handle his social platforms. These solutions may sound obvious from the outside, but when you're stuck in that mental chaos, it can blind you from what actions you should be taking. This is why stopping to get it all out, processing what is happening and figuring out the best path may be exactly what you need to alleviate the overwhelm of what needs to be done.

Other ways to handle overwhelm

If you still feel overwhelmed, then you may need to:

- Implement the right processes to delegate and remove work from your plate.
- Make new hires or offload certain responsibilities to another member of your team.
- Commit to not getting involved in busy work or any task that is outside your zone of genius.
- Be diligent in auditing what you're doing, planning your days and defending your time.
- Double down on self-care practices like meditation, breathing, exercise or disconnecting from devices to allow yourself to manage stress.
- Simply take a break, remove yourself from your environment and allow yourself to calm down. When you allow yourself to remain in that stressed state, the overwhelm and tension will continue to build up inside you. Whereas if you stepped away, went for a walk, got a drink, or allowed yourself a few minutes to relax, chances are you'll be able to return calm and ready to refocus on what you're doing.

I'm not going to go through how to do all the processes, delegation and time management practices as it's the focus of my book *"The Effective CEO"*. Regardless, if you want to reduce overwhelm, then you have to think like a CEO. That means instead of getting stuck in the trenches or dragged into a state of response, allow yourself time to process what's happening, create an actual plan and remove anything that doesn't need to be done by you. On top of that, also ensure you don't get pulled into stories or allow yourself to be consumed by the thought of what you need to do on step five, when you should be focusing on step one. After all, big goals and targets in themselves can inherently feel overwhelming, which is why breaking them down into smaller steps or targets can make them far clearer and mentally easier to deal with.

On a side note, I find one big struggle my clients have is being able to switch off. Where when they get home, even though they're there physically, mentally they're checked out, thinking about work. This in turn can often leave them feeling disconnected from those around them, or with scattered racing thoughts that keep them awake at night.

That's why I always recommend they end their days by taking 10 to 15 minutes to do the mental brain dump exercise, getting all of their thoughts down on paper and creating a plan for how to handle them. Not only does this put them at ease knowing they have a plan for what needs to get done, it also allows them to disconnect, letting go of many of these racing thoughts and the overwhelm that comes with them. It also goes a long way in ensuring you can effectively plan your days, as you can then revisit these thoughts the following day and use that clarity to determine how to spend your time. This is also the final action I take every Friday afternoon, as doing so allows me to go into the weekend, knowing I can pick up where I left off.

Is this a miracle cure? Of course not. But doing this regularly will have a huge impact on your mental state, especially when combined with all the other shifts and changes you implement from this book. Remember, it's not one single action that will solve your problems. Instead, it's little shifts that when compounded, will transform the way you think, feel and perform.

I know we've covered a lot so far, so you may even want to act on this before you go any further. Take a moment to reflect on everything you've learned so far and create a list of all the tasks and actions you need to take. That way you can ensure you don't forget or overlook anything, and in turn, it'll allow you to feel far more focused and in control of what you need to get done.

If you haven't already, also make sure you download the resources pack, as one of the bonuses I'll share my CEO planning and productivity training. This will show you how you organize what you are doing, maximize your time and transform what you get done in a day. You'll also find other bonuses and training videos to help you take what you learn in this book to the next level.

Access the resources at:
https://www.byronmorrison.com/resources

Trusting your intuition

When the stakes are high or there is huge pressure on you to deliver, it can be easy to fall into a cycle of doubting yourself. I saw this in one of my first time CEO clients, who when we first started working together, had a huge tendency to second-guess himself at every turn. A mental block that would cause him to avoid big decisions for weeks at a time, or to look for hand-holding and approval from his investors as he was terrified to make a mistake. What was more frustrating was that his gut would tell him to take a certain action, but he'd go against it due to the advice of others. Yet more often than not, it would turn out his gut was right all along, causing him to further beat himself up.

If you look at any top leader or CEO, the one thing they all have in common is they surround themselves with the right support. The reason being is that they recognize it's vital to have people around you to advise you on what path of action to take. In fact, this is one of the biggest reasons why clients hire me, as they want someone who is disconnected and a prop that they can lean on, so that they don't have to get into the ring alone. Not only that, but even CEOs need accountability, especially when they have no one to hold them to what they say they'll do.

With that being said, even though I'm obviously a huge proponent of external support, I'd be remiss if I didn't point out that not all advice is equal. Especially since people tend to have an opinion about everything and believe that they're experts in issues they really have no clue about. After all, just log in to Facebook and that old high school friend who last week was an expert in the economy is now a medical expert, politician, or environmental scientist.

Because of that, if you want to think like a CEO, then you have to audit where advice is coming from and how much weight you put on it. It's like when you tell a friend about a business challenge you're having and they start telling you how they'd handle it. Now they may be full of good intentions and believe what they say to be true, but think, where is this advice coming from? Because if they've only ever worked in a corporate job, never run a business or been in the situation you're in, do you really want to take their advice on this topic? Especially since people like to talk a big game, but when the pressure is on or their back is against the wall, they behave entirely differently.

Not only that, you also need to audit where their interests lie. For instance, one of the biggest confrontations I find clients have is with their CFO. The reason being is their job is to protect cash flow and often their advice will be focused on short-term survival over big picture needs. One of my clients was having this constantly, where the CFO would fight him at every turn, over decisions with new hires, marketing campaigns or expenses that he didn't view as "necessary". And this is a good thing! As you need someone like this in your corner to ensure you aren't being reckless and to challenge you so you don't make impulse decisions. But this client was CEO for a reason and ultimately it was on him to make the final decision based on the vision and where he was leading the business. Yet because he was second-guessing himself, he'd often give in. One instance was when the CFO talked him out of hiring a new marketing manager, where even though he was convinced it was the right path, he didn't follow through. A decision that, he realized three months later, was short-sighted and needed to be done anyway, only now that short-term saving on their runway left them three months behind their growth plan.

This is exactly why when clients ask for advice on certain topics, I always remind them to remember where my advice is coming from. After all, my expertise is in mindset, performance and emotional control, not in growing and scaling businesses, hiring or operations (issues we rarely talk about since our focus is on them, not the business).

However, at times, these issues do come up and one of my superpowers is asking the right questions, pulling apart ideas and being a sounding board. Especially since I've been privy to conversations with some incredible CEOs and leaders, and can undoubtedly bring unique perspectives to the table. But regardless, it would be ignorant to proclaim I always have the right answer, which is why I'm always clear in these moments to remind them to take any guidance with a grain of salt.

While I'm aware of this and able to highlight it, most people aren't. Instead, they live in their own little bubble, convinced their thoughts, opinions and beliefs are correct. After all, that's how our brain is programmed, and it comes down to our individual mould of the world. That in itself though is why as a CEO it's vital that with any piece of advice you stop to ask yourself – where is this coming from? Where do this person's interests lie? And do they know all the information and full picture of what's going on?

Another example is taking advice directly from investors or your board. Sure, they may be great resources for guidance and information. But often their main interests will be in boosting revenue or cutting down on costs. Or their advice will be based on what they see, without knowing the full facts, internal struggles, and daily challenges you're going through. One of my clients discovered this the hard way, when for months he faced frustration over following advice that went against his intuition, simply because as a founder and first time CEO, he lacked confidence in himself. Eventually, through our reflections and conversations he realized that even though his investors' intentions were coming from the right place, the reality was that no one knew the product, market, vision, or technology as well as him and his team. Meaning they needed to trust in themselves, as they knew better than anyone why they were making certain decisions or taking particular actions. It was a new way of thinking, one that bolstered his convictions and self-belief.

Now I'm not saying you should dismiss all outside guidance and advice. If anything, it's the opposite. It's just important that before you allow outside influence to guide your decisions, that you fully process where it's coming from.

In short, just make sure you audit where guidance is coming from, as not all advice should be taken at face value or deemed as equal.

Developing your intuition

When it comes to advancing your ability to trust your intuition, a huge part of improving this skill set goes back to self-reflection. To develop your intuition, decision making and convictions, it's essential that you regularly stop to break down situations, how you handled them and what you can learn from them for the future. This is the easiest way to grow and evolve, as not only will this boost your confidence in your own abilities, but you'll also feel far more comfortable in handling similar situations again in the future.

Chances are that whenever your intuition is telling you to go down a certain path, it's probably for a reason. Because of that, one action you can implement is a "gut check" where whenever you feel tension over what you think you should do, stop and ask yourself what is your gut telling you? Why do you feel like you should take that action? And what's pulling you in a different direction? Again, sometimes simply stopping to fully process the situation instead of acting on impulse may be exactly what you need to get out of your own head and determine the right path.

At the end of each day, you may also want to reflect on the key situations where your gut came into play. You'll want to process what thoughts were behind that way of thinking, how the situation played out and what you can learn for the future. All of this will better prepare you to handle similar situations and help you gain the self-awareness needed to understand and trust in yourself.

With that in mind, it's vital to remember that even if you do make a mistake, chances are you can always correct your course or pivot based on new findings or realizations. Which is why in most cases, it's better to act fast (not reckless) based on what you do know, than it is to stall and stay stuck.

Going back to section one, this is why one of the tasks I gave you was to create a table each day to reflect on what went right, what went wrong and what your responsibility was in making it happen. Doing so forces you to stop and take stock of how your day went, allowing you to uncover what you could have done and how to handle similar situations in the future. This is also why with clients I track their progress daily. By doing so, in our sessions we can then break down the biggest challenges they faced, going through everything from how they handled them, to the way they felt and what they could do differently next time.

Not taking time for regular reflection is one of the biggest reasons why overwhelmed CEOs struggle with confidence and doubt themselves. But by making this action a non-negotiable regular task, that's how you'll develop your intuition. In turn, this is what will allow you to take everything from your confidence to your decision-making, how you lead, perform under pressure and your ability to navigate challenges to the next level.

Section 4

Determining what to focus on

A huge part of thinking like a CEO will come down to knowing where to focus your time, when to delegate and how to leverage the time of those around you. Getting this right truly will make the difference between being an Evolved CEO who feels in control of their day, and an overwhelmed CEO who is stretched thin and always feels like they're behind.

Just as a heads up, in this section I'm going to be focusing more on the why and what to do over the how. I covered all of this in "The Effective CEO" and I don't want to simply rehash old work or copy and paste what I said before. If you do want to dive into this further, I'll share a link later in this section for you to check it out.

The reality is that when you're a CEO and running a business, it can feel like there are always a million different things to get done. Which is why most overwhelmed CEOs I speak to tell me that time is the biggest problem they face. Pretty much every time I break down what's going on in their world though, I uncover that the actual issue is something completely different. Now I'm going to share that with you in a moment, but before I do I want to put this into perspective with an example.

When one of my clients first reached out to me, he had so much to do that he was working sixty-plus-hour weeks just to try and get everything done. Yet regardless of how much time he put in, he still felt stretched thin and like he was never able to catch up. I uncovered that because he had so many things to do, he was in the classic overwhelmed CEO cycle of spinning his wheels and unsure what to focus on or prioritize. So he'd bounce around from one task to the next, where one minute he'd be working on a report, then he'd be responding to emails, then he'd be pulled into a meeting.

He was constantly rushing around trying to get things done, to the point that he was barely stopping to breathe, let alone think.

And because he was in this constant state of reaction, he'd get trapped in his own head, battling scattered racing thoughts and overthinking key decisions. A state of mind that was causing him to second guess himself at every turn, which at times had an almost paralyzing effect. So, even though he knew what he should be doing, he'd end up procrastinating, doing "busy" work, or mindlessly scrolling through his newsfeed, avoiding what needed to get done.

Even though he felt "busy," he really wasn't getting much done. Meaning that come the end of the day, he'd regularly have to skip workouts, cancel date night with his wife and work late into the evenings to try and catch up. Because of all this, like so many other overwhelmed CEOs understandably, he thought he had a time problem.

When actually...

He had an effectiveness problem.

As he wasn't making the best use of the time that he had.

That's the problem when you don't evolve as a CEO, as you end up in a world focusing on tasks that shouldn't be taking up your time, pulled into problems that shouldn't be getting your attention and on busy work that isn't driving the business forward. All of which can make you a slave to your business, where instead of living a life of freedom on your terms, you're working endless hours and still feeling like you're running backwards on a treadmill, unable to catch up.

For this client, we audited what he was doing, got him clear on what to focus on and prioritize, and implemented the right systems to delegate everything else. We then focused on getting him out of a state of reaction, so he could control his emotions and get off that rollercoaster ride of ups and downs. Once he was calm and grounded, we broke through the mental blocks that were causing him to doubt and second guess himself. And finally, we installed the right routines to effectively manage his time, plan his days and prioritize what needed to get done. The result? He transformed what he gets done in a day. He took back over 15 hours a week, with less stress and overwhelm. That's 15 hours he can now focus on growing the business, connecting with his family, or enjoying the freedom he worked so hard for.

As you can see, we didn't achieve this by adding more to his plate. And while coming in he believed he had a "time" problem, instead we focused on ensuring he executed at a higher level and made the best use of the time he did have. That was how he took back control.

That's why if you want to think like a CEO, then it's vital to realize that what you don't do, is just as important as what you do do.

In fact, this is so important I'll make it bold and say it again.

If you want to think like a CEO, then it's vital to realize that what you don't do, is just as important as what you do do.

After all, every hour you waste on reactionary problems, tasks that don't matter or being stuck in your own head is an hour you could be spending on creating more revenue, more growth and more impact. Or it's an hour you could be spending with your family and enjoying life.

A call with one of my clients a few months ago illustrated this perfectly. When we got on the phone, I could tell something was wrong. His energy was off, he seemed tense and not his usual self. When I asked what was going on, he started telling me about how he was stressing over sorting his travel arrangements and itinerary for a business trip the next week.

Now the reason this was problematic, was in a few days he had a huge pitch that could be a turning point for the business. Yet his focus and attention were on his travel, instead of what he needed to prepare for his presentation. Sure, booking the transport would probably only take an hour. But he was losing hours of mental energy and bandwidth from the stress of trying to figure out everything he needed to arrange. Worst still, a few months ago he hired an assistant to handle tasks exactly like this. He just hadn't thought to hand it off.

This is why if you want to think like a CEO, you have to audit what you're currently doing, figuring out anything that is outside your "zone of genius" and removing it. When I talk about "zone of genius", I mean the high growth tasks that can only be done by you and responsibilities that have the greatest ROI for your time.

Here's another way to think of it. Let's say your time is worth $500 an hour. In that case, you should not be doing any tasks that you could pay someone else to do, for considerably less than that $500 amount. You wouldn't pay someone $500 to organise your inbox or run company errands, so why should you do it? Going back to the client sorting his travel, every hour he wasted on tasks he could pay his $15 an hour assistant to do, is losing him money. Meaning that task needs to be delegated or handed off so that instead he can prioritize tasks that make the best use of his time.

In my book *"The Effective CEO"* I give another example from an application call where the CEO was losing an hour a day to distractions. At the time it was nothing more than a minor frustration, but in the bigger context after our conversation, he realized this was costing him $1,500 a day! That's $7,500 a week! And $390,000 a year!

That's why there are no two ways about it, you simply have to figure out where your time has the greatest impact and from there delegate or let go of everything else.

How to audit what you're doing

I'm not going through the entire process of how to do this as it's all laid out in "*The Effective CEO*", but in short, the 5-step process to audit what you're doing and determine what takes up your time is:

1) Create a list of everything that needs to get done.

2) Ask yourself, is this actually important? If no, remove it.

3) If yes, does it fall into your 90-day targets? If yes, it stays. If no, add it to your "Idea Bank" spreadsheet.

4) Does this need to be done by you? If yes, it stays.

5) If no, who do you need to delegate, outsource, or hand it over to?

These are five questions I highly advise adding into your weekly planning, as they will go a long way towards helping you determine what to focus on and what needs to be removed or delegated to someone else. Remember that being a highly effective CEO is not about getting a million things done. Instead, it's about bringing together the right team, leveraging the skills of others and steering the ship. This realization though, is one that few overwhelmed CEOs come to, as instead, they tend to micromanage everything, put too much on their plate and struggle letting go.

Now, if you know what you should delegate but don't because you fear the team will drop the ball or no one else can do it as well as you can, then that in itself is a mental block you need to work on. Because when someone says this to me, it generally is for one of two reasons:

1) They haven't given their team the opportunity to step up.

2) They haven't hired the right people.

If it's the latter, then that is an entirely separate issue and one in which it unfortunately, rests on you as a CEO to trim the fat and build a team who can competently add value to the business. However, if you have hired the right people but simply haven't let go, then it's important to remember that not giving them the opportunity to step up isn't just doing them a disservice, it's also doing you, the team, your customers and the business a disservice as well.

Now, I know letting go may be scary, but the only way you are ever going to grow is to pull off the band-aid and let the people you hired to do their job. And sure, initially, there probably will be mistakes and a learning curve will need to be faced. But long-term, this is going to solve far more headaches than it creates. Especially when it frees you up to focus on high-value work or tasks that can only be done by you.

I had this conversation with a client a few months ago who, when we started working together, was a massive micromanager, getting involved in every area of her business and refusing to give the ball to her team. Once I put this into perspective for her and she decided to have faith and let go, her entire life and business changed. She found she had some amazing people, who brought in some incredible ideas and took control of owning what needed to get done. As a result, she's far less involved and no longer feels like everything rests on her shoulders. Recently she even took a couple of weeks' break, free from stress, as she knew her team could handle what needed to get done. This only happened because she made a decision to stop thinking like a manager, and instead, start thinking like a CEO. After all, if you want to create a huge company that changes and impacts the world, then you need to trust in those around you, as you will never be able to do everything yourself.

Again, in "*The Effective CEO*" I go through all of this, so I don't want to repeat it all now. One useful exercise to do though is to sit down and create a list of everything you did over the last couple of weeks, going through it and honestly asking what could only have been done by you? What was busy work? And what should have been done by someone else? In doing so, look for reoccurring tasks and trends, along with anything that in future that needs to be done by someone else. Remember, this is all about bringing into your awareness how and where you're spending your time.

Then, from there, look at your current to-do list and do exactly the same thing. Being honest about what can and should only be done by you, and what needs to be given to someone else. Getting this right will go a long way to protecting your own mindset and energy, allowing you instead to prioritize what needs to be done and emerge as the CEO your company needs you to become.

Once you have this clarity, it's then vital you use it to effectively plan and manage your time. To help you do exactly that, I've put together a training breaking down the entire planning process I teach my private clients. I'll show you how to properly plan your days, weeks and months, structure your time, reflect on what you got done and ensure you can prioritize key drivers of growth. You can watch the training in the resources pack. If you haven't already, download at:

www.byronmorrison.com/resources

The ever evolving role

It's important to note, that chances are your roles and responsibilities are likely to change and grow along with your business. Which is why this clarity is not a once and done thing, and instead it needs to be a regular part of your reflection. After all, tasks and responsibilities that currently lead to growth, could six months from now, be holding you back.

This was a discovery made by one of my clients, who initially grew his business from networking events and meeting other people. Yet, over the last few years, their business had pivoted, they'd automated the majority of their marketing and were serving a completely different market. Meaning that, for the clients they were catering for now, networking was ineffective. The thing is though, because he was so used to attending these events, he hadn't stopped to question whether he actually should continue to do so. To make matters worse, he absolutely hated getting up early to attend these meetings. Not only that, it also left him tired and unfocused for the rest of the day, taking his bandwidth away from work that actually mattered. It was only when we stopped to audit what he was doing that he uncovered that these weekly events were now having a hugely negative ROI. This newfound clarity was the permission he needed to let go of those tasks. In turn, freeing him up to make better use of his time.

Chances are you too will have tasks, responsibilities, or regular actions you take that you shouldn't be spending your time or attention on. Or that once were profitable or necessary, yet now are a waste of time and resources. Which is why I'll say it again...

If you want to think like a CEO, then it's vital to realize that what you don't do, is just as important as what you do do.

With that in mind, take some time to audit what you're doing. Figure out what's the best use of your time. And let go of anything that is taking you away from focusing on what you need to do.

It's important to note that this applies to every area of your life. Based off this audit, I've had clients hire cleaners, sign up for meal delivery services, hire personal assistants and outsource other chores that took up their time and bandwidth. All because they realized the time and energy going into these tasks were taking them away from what they should be doing. In turn, freeing them up to focus on what matters and enjoy their life.

Because of that, always make sure that whenever you audit and reflect on what you're doing, you're always approaching it from a holistic viewpoint. Get this right, and it'll transform what you can get done in a day, along with amplifying everything from your focus to your productivity and overall state of mind.

I know this section was short and to the point, but if you do want to dive into how to hone your focus, maximize your days and take control of your role, then you can grab a copy of "*The Effective CEO*" at:

https://byronmorrison.com/theeffectiveceo

Section 5

Leading like a CEO

A central part of being an effective CEO will come down to knowing how to communicate with your team, inspire others and bring out the best in those around you. After all, great businesses aren't just built by one person and instead they rely on amazing people coming together to create something bigger than themselves.

Leadership as a theme could easily fill this book by itself and while it is a component of what we are discussing, it is only a small piece of the overall theme. Because of that, I'm going to hone our focus to four key areas and strategies that I believe are vital parts of thinking like a CEO. Implement these shifts and you'll be able to authentically connect with those around you, create an environment where people feel heard and deal with challenges before they spiral out of control.

Speak less, listen more

A few months ago, I started working with a client who was in the process of growing a SAAS tech start-up. Coming from a real estate background, he was not only new to the industry, he was also completely new to the role of CEO. Because of that, he found himself leading a global team, along with a host of responsibilities he'd never previously been exposed to.

He believed that as CEO, it was on him to lead meetings, express his ideas and tell people exactly what they were doing (even if he wasn't fully sure himself). This left him unaware that his desire to portray the image of a strong decisive leader, was actually doing more harm than good. Especially since he was making decisions based on short-sighted information, missing opportunities to understand the full picture and not allowing the team he hired to fully contribute to their full potential.

Upon discovering this trait, I challenged him to change his perspectives on not just what the role involved, but also how to approach dealing with people. Because here's the thing – as CEO, it's not on you to know everything or be involved in every detail. Instead, it's on you to surround yourself with the best people, gather their ideas and then use that to take decisive action on leading the business.

That's why a real leader is not the person who speaks first or the loudest, and instead, it's the person who speaks last. The reason being is when you go into meetings or situations and immediately start dictating what is happening, you miss out on a host of new opportunities. Instead, by setting the agenda and allowing the team to speak first, two things happen:

1) You open the floor for people to express new opinions and bring ideas to the table. And sure, you probably have an idea of the outcome you want to create, but you may have missed certain details or be unaware of factors that could completely change the plan or approach. If you had gone ahead and expressed your thoughts, these details probably would have been overlooked, especially if people don't want to suggest paths of action that go against your thinking. Also, by you illustrating your thoughts first, you run the risk of moulding the team's views and ideas, creating biased solutions, which again can potentially cause you to miss out on alternative viewpoints.

2) Once you've gathered all these insights, thoughts and opinions, it will then put you in a far stronger position to fully understand what's happening and from there, to make a decision on what to do about it. Missing out on this and cementing your thoughts without this information will often

be short-sighted and nowhere near as concise as it could have been otherwise.

Obviously, this isn't how to approach every meeting, as there will be times when it's on you to lead, show the strategy and express what's happening. However, by creating more opportunities where you speak less and listen more, you'll open yourself up to a whole new realm of ideas, giving your team a voice and empowering them to step up and do the job you hired them for in the first place. Or as the Dalai Lama put it "when you talk, you are only repeating what you already know. But if you listen, you may learn something new."

Getting your team on board

One of my clients came to one of our calls incredibly frustrated by the fact that no matter what she tried, she simply couldn't get her team on the same page. Instead, she felt like she was in a never-ending battle in a toxic environment, where no one took responsibility for their actions and blamed everyone else whenever something went wrong.

The purpose of the team in question was to bring in new students, which involved them making phone calls, attending events and meeting with potential candidates. To keep on top of everything, she kept trying to install a system of accountability, where every day people would check in with their progress, share what they had done and keep everyone updated with their actions. She perceived this as the best possible system to track their progress, monitor the team's performance and ensure they hit their targets. Yet no matter how hard she tried, people refused and fought her at every turn.

Despite her knowing the outcome she wanted to create, it was clear her standing up in the team meetings and telling people what to do wasn't working. What I reminded her of is that on a basic psychological level - no one likes being told what to do. If anything, it immediately puts them on the defence, where even if it's the correct action, they'll resent having to follow through.

Not only that, but the problem with her addressing the team and telling them what to do was positioning her against them. Now, you can argue all you want that because she's in charge people should listen and do what she said. Unfortunately, people inherently aren't that simple and at times, getting through to them requires a different approach. With that in mind, I suggested she flipped what she was doing, where instead of it being a "her against them" situation, she created a common (for lack of a better word) "enemy" where they were on the same side. In this case – the board. What this meant was that rather than starting the next meeting saying what she wanted, she led with: "these are the targets the board have set for us". By framing the situation in this way, it immediately pulled her and the team into alignment. From there, instead of telling them how they were going to make it happen, she stepped back, and said: "how do you think we should approach this?".

In her mind, the answer was obvious, and she knew the outcome she wanted. But by putting the solution in the hands of the team she removed the confrontation and instead, she could ask leading questions that would build towards the outcome.

For instance, an employee could respond with "we need to make 'x' amount of calls a day". She could then ask her "how can we monitor that progress and make sure we're on track?" Or "what support do you need?" All of a sudden, the employee had suggested making the calls and checking in daily with the team so that everyone is on the same page; the exact outcome this client had been fighting for months to achieve. Yet now her employees believed it was their idea, and because they had suggested it, they could now be held accountable for their actions, especially if they didn't follow through.

When you coach and guide people towards realizations in a non-manipulative way, their entire mentality changes. As a result, this client was able to create an environment where people supported each other and stuck to what they needed to do. All by allowing them the opportunity to feel like they contributed. By doing so, targets were hit, accountability practices were put in place and a cohesive unit was formed, all by repositioning the perceived problem and creating a feeling that they were all working towards a common goal.

Going back to the first point of speaking less and listening more, by opening up the floor for the team to speak, this client also gained new insights and ways to approach their targets she never thought about. Meaning that by having a rough idea of the outcome and asking leading questions, she was able to gain invaluable ideas, including better ways to execute the check-in process and track their outreach. Many of which had been overlooked in the weeks she'd previously spent fighting against the team and trying to get them to do what she said.

It's important to note that approaching situations in this way is not about manipulation. Instead, it's about bringing out the best in your people and creating an environment where they feel heard. Another great example of this is coaching – a practice you'll probably either experience yourself, or have to do to support your team. Often when coaching someone, you'll have conversations where from the outside, the solution may seem glaringly obvious. But if you just told the person the answer, you're taking away the growth they gain in mentally processing the situation and reaching the conclusion. Which is why instead, it's on you to ask the right questions and guide them to figuring out the best path of action.

Not only that, but this is also where you need to check your ego at the door, as the worst thing you can do is get frustrated or rush the process, simply because you think the answer is clear. Because here's the thing - even though you may think you know the solution, there is always the possibility that you're wrong, you've missed something, or that there's a better way to achieve the result. That's why whether you're the coach or the client, you'll achieve far more by having a safe space to explore ideas, challenge perceptions and explore new potential outcomes.

On a side note – regardless as to whether you're running a meeting or having a one-to-one conversation, if you want to think like a CEO, then you have to be clear on the outcomes and targets you're trying to create. I see this all the time in new clients where not having this in place leads to one of their biggest frustrations in wasting time in meetings that go off track or end up achieving nothing. In most cases, this could simply have been avoided if there was a clear plan and agenda in place. With that in mind, I encourage all my clients, before all major meetings, to get clear on what they want to get out of the time. Yes, it requires more work, but that five to ten minutes to plan could save an hour in wasted time. By having this insight, you can then go into meetings, set a clear agenda and desired outcome, and then course correct the conversation anytime it starts to drift off track. This is how you ensure the time is focused and effectively used. Going beyond that, it's also vital to reflect on how the meeting went and what you can learn about navigating similar situations in the future.

I saw this on a client call where after a board meeting, the CEO was frustrated that he didn't know the answers to several key questions. In this case, he had planned for what he wanted to cover, but he hadn't stopped to ask himself what the outcome he wanted was or what follow up questions could be asked. In hindsight, that would have allowed him to reverse engineer the journey, factoring in certain elements into his plan that would have made the meeting with the board far more constructive. With that in mind, when planning ask yourself what is the purpose of this meeting? What outcome do I want to create? What would it look like if the meeting was a success? What potential questions, objections or concerns might I need to address? This planning doesn't need to take long, but your clarity can completely change what you focus on, the points you present and the questions you ask.

This is another example of where mindset is so key to success. This client came into our call frustrated and beating himself up over what he didn't do. I reminded him that no amount of focusing on the past could undo what happened, but as frustrating as this situation was, it was also a huge positive, as it showed him what to do in the future. Meaning even though it may not have felt like it in the moment, it was actually a win. Once we put it into perspective, it became far easier to let it go and move on.

I said this earlier, but as it's the central theme of this book, I'll say it again. Even though mistakes or setbacks may be painful, they are also your greatest opportunity for growth. After all, it is in those times that you learn what not to do, how to improve and how to handle situations better in the future. All of which is clarity you never would have received if things went "ok". I know in those times it's easy to dwell on the past or beat yourself up, which is why it's vital you shift your focus to the future, what you can learn and what you're going to do about it.

Facing challenging conversations

If you're anything like the clients who come to me for help, then one of your biggest challenges is probably avoiding confrontations and difficult conversations. I get it, it's uncomfortable and places you in situations that you'd rather not be in. However, these responsibilities come with the role and avoiding them not only delays the inevitable, it can also bring a host of new problems.

When I first met one of my clients, he admitted he had a member of his team that he wanted to fire six months ago. Yet even though he knew what needed to be done, as a first time CEO who had never fired someone before, he just couldn't bring himself to face that conversation. In the six months this issue was left unresolved, huge problems began to manifest. Mistakes were made with clients, frustrations were built within the team and during a period of limited runway, further expense was wasted on his salary. Not only that, but failing to deal with this underperforming employee also placed a huge mental strain on this client to the point it was keeping him awake at night. This problem wasn't going to go away or solve itself, meaning that continuing to avoid it simply created further stress and aggravation – all of which could have been prevented.

If you need another way to look at this, then you can also think that it's also unfair to the employee, as it allowed them to flounder in an environment rather than letting them find what they should be doing. In fact, that was exactly the case when this client eventually faced this conversation, as the employee thanked him for his honesty and agreed the role wasn't the right fit. Meaning they could come to terms and happily part ways.

Now obviously that won't always be the case, but regardless as to whether it's a disciplinary, bringing up feedback, raising issues, or any other situation that could be viewed as a difficult conversation – it will need to be dealt with eventually, which why it's always better to face it sooner than to delay.

It's important to note that fear of facing a challenging conversation directly links to what we discussed in the first half of this book. Where mentally, you go straight to a story, playing out a future worst-case scenario in your mind and convincing yourself about how awful it'll be. Like when you convince yourself that difficult conversation will turn into someone breaking down in tears or losing their temper. The reality is you never truly know how people will react, as while some may get defensive, others will take it in their stride, view the situation as constructive or even as an opportunity to improve. After all, have you ever had a boss or mentor bring up an issue you were unaware of, giving you the opportunity to take that clarity and improve? Remember, not all difficult conversations need to be negative, and instead, they can create a deeper understanding, connection and growth. While bringing them up may be uncomfortable, as long as you approach them in the right way or enter into them with the best intentions, everything will one way or another work out how it is supposed to.

This is also where being proactive comes in. If you believe based on past history or the situation that the conversation is likely to escalate, then you can prepare for it accordingly. Take some time to play it out in your mind, taking yourself through all the scenarios, figuring out how you'd handle them as the best version of yourself. By doing so, if and when that situation does arise, instead of you being put on the spot or reacting, you'll have a game plan for how to respond. This again will go a long way to empowering you to feel confident, as often mistakes are made or emotions take over when we're unprepared for the challenge.

Regardless of what the conversation is, the longer you avoid it, the worse the situation will become. Especially when the runaway stories and fear causes all that anxious energy to build up inside you, which at times can have an almost paralysing effect. The thing is though – even if the worst-case scenario is true and it does turn into an uncomfortable situation, it needs to be dealt with eventually. Which is why as much as you may hate this part of the role, unfortunately, this comes with the territory and it's part of the life that you signed up for. That doesn't mean you need to enjoy it, but it does mean you need to embrace it.

To break through this mental block this client and I came to an agreement where whenever he needed to have a difficult conversation, he'd either do it immediately, or schedule it for as soon as possible. Not only did this allow problems to be solved faster, doing so also freed up his bandwidth, as he'd no longer be wasting energy worrying about problems he was avoiding.

After a while, he started to see these conversations really weren't a big deal and with every situation he faced, his confidence grew. It's reached the point now where he just faces these challenges head-on, without even stopping to think about them. In a recent session, he made a joke that he feels like he doesn't have difficult conversations anymore and he's not sure if it's because it's the stage the business is at, or because he's just so used to handling them. In the 18-months since we started working together, the business has grown, they're focused on entering international markets, have an expanding team and are primed for a huge breakthrough. So I'd be willing to bet it's the latter.

When you handle these situations can be just as important as how you do them. For instance, another client has become far more proficient in facing challenging conversations. Yet in our recent session, he had some internal tension about how he dealt with a situation earlier that week. A member of his team dropped the ball and made a huge mistake, so because of that he called him into his office and reprimanded him. Which was a huge win, especially since in the past, he would have avoided this or put it off.

The issue though, was he had the disciplinary conversation after a team meeting where this problem was raised. Meaning several people thought he let it slide and raised concerns with him later that the employee wasn't facing consequences for his actions, as they didn't know about the follow-up conversation. This caused internal tension, as the CEO was battling whether or not he was sending the wrong message by not reprimanding the employee in the meeting. Especially since he recognized that sometimes as CEO, you need to put your foot down and stand your ground to illustrate that oversights like this can't and won't be tolerated.

While I completely agreed, I told him that some of the best advice I've ever received is "never embarrass someone in public when you can do it in private". As if he had done it in the meeting, the employee likely would have got defensive, justifying his actions and leading to a huge argument. A reality he knew based on the team's history and how much ego came into play whenever it came to disagreements.

With that in mind, based on what happened I suggested a middle ground. Where the next time he was in that situation he could say something along the lines of "something obviously went wrong here, and we need to sit down and discuss this. I'll arrange a time with you to do so after the meeting". This in turn would communicate to the rest of the team that he was handling the issue, as well as allowing him to deal with it as the best version of himself. Especially since he didn't want to be that short-tempered CEO who berates others or fires from the hip simply to try and illustrate a point. This path of action only became clear though from reflecting on the situation, figuring out what worked and how better to handle it in the future.

Regardless, whether it's facing difficult conversations, conflicts or actions, dealing with this goes back to section one. If you have something you know you need to do, put yourself at cause, focus on what you need to do and take action. Commit to either facing it immediately, or scheduling it for as soon as possible. I know it's not easy, but every time you face that fear your confidence will improve. A mentality that will be amplified once you reflect on how you handled the situation and uncover lessons on what to do the next time you need to navigate a similar situation. If you still hesitate, then revisit what we spoke about in the order of consequences and look at the full picture of what your inaction can cause. It sounds simple, but at times despite the fear, like a bungee jumper, you just need to take the leap.

I saw this with another client where their development of their MVP has dragged out to the point it was six months overdue. The business itself is pre-funding, meaning he is financing the entire development himself at a cash rate burn of over $25k a month. This simply wasn't sustainable, especially since development had been going on for a year and a half. As uncomfortable as it may have been, he needed to set a deadline for when they'd be ceasing development and taking their initial offering to market. The thought alone was eating him up inside, as this meant cutting their funding and in many cases, letting team members go until they brought in customers to support further additions to their software. Because of that, he'd been putting it off, allowing the situation to drag on for three months longer than he should have. In the end, his team understood and together they were able to create a plan to speed up development, without further cash burn. Getting everyone on the same page and ensuring the team understood the situation and together they could focus on a way forward.

The reality is, conversations like this are never going to be easy, but unfortunately, they are part of the role. Which is why if you want to be a CEO, you simply have to make the tough decisions, face the difficult situations and make calls that others wouldn't be able to.

It's important to note that whether it is being more effective at leading meetings, getting the team on board, or facing difficult conversations, the reason why the clients listed above were able to get these challenges under control was because of one reason – we tracked what was happening and regularly reflected on and broke down the ins and outs of these situations. Prior to doing so, they had been repeating the same actions for months, where even though they were frustrated by the situation, they were unaware of how to handle the problems or deal with them. By us monitoring what was happening then creating an environment where they could then revisit what happened, dissect how they dealt with the situation and uncover the biggest learnings, that was how they could determine what to do in the future. With that in mind, if you haven't fully embraced or started the tasks I set for you in section one, I highly advise revisiting those points. Especially since that's where the real opportunities for growth and transformation lie. After all, you can read books, do courses, or engulf yourself in personal development all you want, but the biggest lessons will always come from reflecting on your performance and figuring out how to better handle the same situations in the future.

Transparency

A few months ago, I had a fascinating call with one of my mentors. He's ranked as one of the top salespeople in the world and is a fountain of knowledge with over 50 years of experience. When he talks, you can't help but listen. On our call we were discussing some of the biggest challenges faced by CEOs and the key skills they need to succeed. For him, one of the biggest was transparency.

When it comes to thinking like a CEO, transparency and support can be looked at in two different ways, so in the context of leadership, I think it's important we look at both.

The first is that as a CEO, it's not your job to do everything, and instead, it's about bringing together the right people to create the results you want. Unfortunately, this is where so many overwhelmed CEOs become their own worst enemy, as they try to do everything on their own and view asking for help as a weakness. The reality though, is that asking for help is actually a strength. Especially since trusting your team and ensuring you get the right support is one of the most important traits of a great leader. For instance, if you're working on a project and it's touching on finances, but that's not your zone of genius, then trying to wing it or figure it out by yourself is probably going to take longer, all while risking avoidable mistakes. But by putting aside your ego and being transparent in what you need help with, you can then ensure you have the right support. In this case, that may mean asking your CFO to attend a meeting or to take ownership of certain deliverables.

The second area of transparency is about dealing with the isolation of being a CEO. The reality is that running a business can be a pretty lonely life, especially when everyone's looking to you to solve their problems or putting you up on a pedestal as someone who has it all figured out. I find that this situation can lead many overwhelmed CEOs to bottle up their feelings in an effort to not let others see that their internal state doesn't match their external success. I've lost count of how many times I've got on introduction calls with new potential clients, only for them to end up admitting they've never told anyone about these problems. I get it completely, which is why if you're feeling that way, then you're not alone. Carrying that burden though is always going to have huge ramifications, not just in your level of stress, but also how you think, feel and react.

If you look at any top CEO, athlete, or leader who has evolved to their highest level though, what's one thing they all have in common? It's not how hard they work, how much money they've made, or even some super zen meditation technique. Sure, all of these can be important. But the one thing all these top leaders have in common is that they recognize the need to have outside counsel through good times and bad. After all, regardless of how good they are at their job, they need people around them that they can turn to, who have their best interests in mind and who challenge them to think differently or approach problems in new ways. It's the same reason why top athletes hire the right coaches before they win championships, as they recognize the need to have someone who can bring out their best.

That's why I truly believe that if you want to consistently perform at the highest level, then it's vital to have someone in your corner. Someone who can create a place that's a safe and judgment-free zone where you can get these thoughts off your chest, vent and recalibrate. Whether that's a therapist, counsellor, coach or someone like myself, I really encourage you to find someone you trust who can help you get out of your own head. Never underestimate the power in simply having someone to talk to. If that's something you do potentially want my help with, along with pushing you to grow, breaking down challenges and ensuring you can consistently perform at your best, then drop me a message at **byron@byronmorrison.com** and let's see if I can help.

Section 6

Taking this to the next level

If you were to rate where you are right now on a scale of 1 to 10 as far as being able to tap into your full potential, where would you rate yourself? There's no right or wrong, but what number on a scale of 1 to 10 would you give yourself?

Got it?

Keeping that in mind, a few months ago, I was watching a video from one of my mentors and in it he talked about how at a Tony Robbins event his girlfriend was sat next to Oprah at the first event of his she attended. It's important to note that Oprah is worth $2.6 billion, which is even more impressive if you look at her journey and how much the deck was stacked against her. At that event, Tony asked the same question that I just asked you: If you were to rate where you are right now on a scale of 1 to 10 as far as being able to tap into your full potential, where would you rate yourself?

His girlfriend turned to Oprah and said, "I bet that's an easy 10 for you." Can you guess what she replied with?

It wasn't 10.

It was...

3.

Despite her success and all the amazing things she'd done, she knew there is so much more to achieve. Chances are as a CEO or business leader you're already successful, but the question is, what's the next level for you? Because there is always something more.

So let me ask you again.

If you were to rate where you are right now on a scale of 1 to 10 as far as being able to tap into your full potential, where would you rate yourself?

Because if you're anything like myself or the CEO and business leader clients I work with, then what drives you is probably creating an impact all while living a life of freedom on terms. The problem though, is that with every new level of success, comes a new level of problems, which is why so often we can find ourselves in the opposite situation.

I find this table sums it up perfectly:

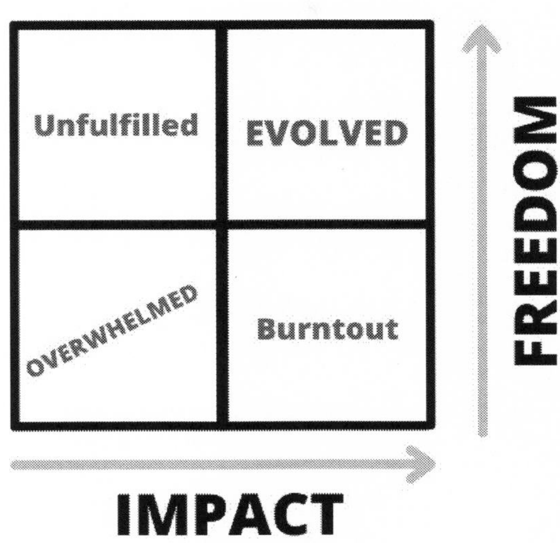

Because as a CEO, in your business you probably want freedom and impact. But when you're stuck in a state of reaction and not focusing on tasks that drive the business forward, you have no freedom and nowhere close to the impact you want. Instead, you're left feeling overwhelmed by everything that needs to get done.

If you have impact, but very little freedom, then you're stretched thin, working 60-hour weeks and burnt out. Or if you've got lots of freedom but no impact, that's when you're unfulfilled. Because of that, the sweet spot is when you have impact, but also freedom to enjoy life.

That's what we call the Evolved CEO - the CEO who feels in control of their life and business and who is living a life on their terms.

The problem that most people don't realize though, is that growth, can actually be a huge trap. Most CEOs aren't aware that a CEO just starting out will generally have more control than a CEO with a successful business (this doesn't have to be the case, but it often is).

The reason being is simple - the new level of problems that come with every new level of success. Especially when you have a growing team. You have more stakeholders to keep happy. You have more operations and moving parts. And that's before you add in all the fires, solving everyone else's problems and dealing with never-ending demands.

When you're in this situation, what lands up happening is you take on more responsibilities. You work longer hours. You put more pressure on yourself. And as a result, you land up pushing yourself harder. And sure, the business will continue to grow. But you'll land up dreading anytime the phone rings. You'll resent your team every time they ask for help on a problem they should know how to handle. Worst of all, you'll stop enjoying your business, as it'll be a never-ending mental and emotional drain. Yet you'll keep telling yourself that once you reach the next level it'll be easier. That then you'll let go, you'll have more time, you'll feel more in control.

That's why I call this the "overwhelmed CEO trap". As that next level just brings more challenges, problems and demands. I've been there myself, which is why I know exactly how this feels. And unfortunately, this is why most CEOs become the bottleneck, as they're so pulled into the day to day of the business, that they're actually the ones who get in the way. Which in turn, causes them to fall short of the impact, income and success they could create.

How do you avoid this happening?

Over the last few years from working with and studying some of the top CEOs from around the world, I discovered that the CEOs and business leaders who had not only reached the top of the mountain, but were able to sustain their success as well, had mastered three key areas: their mindset, emotional control and performance. By evolving within themselves, this was how they unlocked the ability to show up as a confident and powerful leader who can make timely decisions, handle the stress of running a business and inspire those around them. This was how they became that next level, evolved CEO.

Now, the purpose of this book has been all about helping you think like a CEO, showing you how to stop reacting, breakthrough mental blocks and consistently take the actions you need to take. Everything I've shared with you has been tried and tested, and it works, as long as you implement these tools and follow through.

Have you ever thought about why you can give 100 people the exact same strategy, yet they all get vastly different results?

If the strategy's the same, then what's the difference?

The biggest differences are the mindset and emotional control of the person trying to execute the strategy. After all, the perfect strategy or plan is meaningless if you're spending your days in a reactive state, stressed and overwhelmed, or if you're overthinking decisions, doubting yourself and not having the confidence to execute on what you need to get done.

This is where so many overwhelmed CEOs get caught in the trap of focusing on the wrong areas of growth. Convincing themselves the reason why things aren't working is because they have the wrong strategy, or because they need more tactics. I'll be the first to admit how much I fell into this trap in the past, as I spent so much time bouncing around between books, courses and training programs, hoping I'd find the magical secret that would turn it all around. It was only when I stopped and did the inner deep work that I realized the biggest barrier in the way, was myself. It was that sabotaging voice in my head and my inability to deal with the challenges that came with my success. This was the real reason why my role felt out of my control.

Obviously having the right strategy is important, but what I found was that the Evolved CEOs who recognize the need to grow within themselves by building an internal foundation around the three core pillars of mindset, emotional control and performance were the ones who are able to take those strategies and execute them at the highest level. It's what gives them their edge and enables them to consistently show up at their best, all while keeping it together in the face of adversity.

That's because each pillar directly impacts the others:

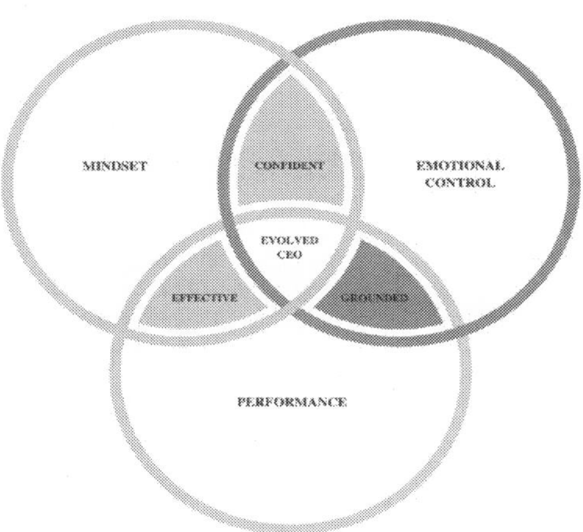

What I've found is that most overwhelmed CEOs tend to just focus on one or possibly two of these pillars. This is a huge issue, because:

- You can have the right mindset and be super productive, but if you can't control the stress or deal with the pressure, it's going to keep you trapped in a reactive state of fight or flight where you're controlled by your emotions.

- Or you can be organized and grounded, but if you don't believe in yourself, then you'll keep second-guessing what you're doing, avoiding making decisions and not taking the actions you know you need to take.

- Or you can mentally and emotionally be in the right place, but if you don't know how to manage and defend your time, then you'll spend your days stretched thin and feeling like no matter what you do, you're always behind.

Now, if your role currently feels out of your control and you're not performing at the level that you want, I'd be willing to bet you're missing one or more of these pillars. That's why to become an Evolved CEO, we need to build a foundation of all three. Because when you get them in alignment, that's when you'll be able to tap into your full potential. This is how you evolve into that next level, more confident, grounded and effective decision-making leader, who can handle the pressures of running and growing a business.

It's important to note, that ensuring these foundations are built and strengthened becomes even more important as your business grows. After all, with every new level of success, comes a new level of problems, which is why the level of thinking, emotional control and performance that got you to where you are now, isn't going to be enough to sustain this level of success, let alone breakthrough to the next level.

Think of it like a house. The first thing they focus on strengthening is the foundation, as they know that's what will keep it grounded and strong. This becomes even more important if they want to add more levels on top, as the taller that building becomes, the stronger the foundation needs to be. That's how you ensure you don't crumble, helping you not just survive, but thrive at the highest level.

Where do we go from here

This book has been the first step in the journey. But with that being said, this has very much been the tip of the iceberg in regards to what we can do. Because of that, if you want to take it to the next level, then I may be able to help.

Because imagine this...

Imagine waking up in 90-days and from the moment you start your day instead of feeling overwhelmed by a never-ending to-do list, knowing exactly what to focus on and prioritize. With the right systems in place to manage your time, effectively delegate and ensure that instead of getting stuck in your own head, you can consistently take the actions you need to take.

Imagine having the clear-headed focus to make better decisions and the confidence to know that regardless of the challenge in front of you, that you can handle it and get through. Where even if things do go wrong, you can trust your own intuition, stay emotionally stable and despite the chaos going on around you, remain calm, have clarity and feel in control.

Imagine that rather than your days consumed by fires or reacting to problems, that you could get out of the trenches and finally step into the role of the CEO you need to become to take your business to the next level. Where you can reflect on your days knowing that the work you did grew the business, furthered your vision and created more revenue and impact.

Imagine feeling in control of your life and business. Where when you do take time off you can be present, feel connected to those around you and finally enjoy the freedom you worked so hard for.

And imagine that instead of feeling like you were in this on your own, you had someone in your corner and a prop that you could lean on so that you don't have to get into the ring alone.

Because here's the thing. You don't need to imagine this happening, as I want to help you turn this into a reality.

From everything we've covered in this book, do you think that if you spent the next few months, or even 12 months with me coaching you, do you think that would have a positive impact on your performance as a CEO, your life and the success that you could create?

If the answer is yes, then there are two options. If you want support working directly with me, then my Evolved program may be a great fit. Alternatively, if you'd rather do it on your own, then my Unshakeable course will take you step by step through everything you need to know.

Both will help you take control of your role so that you can break through to the next level. The big difference obviously, is the amount of direct support you receive. I'll give you an overview of both, and from there you can decide which path is right for you.

The Evolved program

I developed the Evolved program for CEOs who want to become more effective in their role. Using my battle-tested 5-step Evolved Method, I want to evolve you into the CEO your business needs to break through to the next level of success.

Because does this sound like the situation you're in right now?

- You're feeling stretched thin, overloaded and overwhelmed by everything that needs to get done
- You have so many competing priorities that you often get stuck spinning your wheels or doing tasks that don't lead to growth
- You're highly reactive and a lot of your days are spent putting out fires and dealing with other people's problems
- You get times where you overthink, second guess yourself, struggle making decisions and procrastinate, avoiding what you know you need to do
- You're not clearly communicating, setting expectations or keeping people accountable
- You struggle with balance and even when you do take time off you're attached to phone thinking about work

If this sounds like you, then I want to help you get this under control. Working directly with me, I'll help you change the way you think, how you process problems, navigate challenges, manage people and perform in your role. By the end, you'll be able to maximize your time, lead with confidence and grow a business without losing your sanity.

Just a few of the things we'll do include:

- Figure out what you need to prioritize then implement the right processes to effectively delegate, manage your workload, defend your time and maximize what you can get done

- Up-level your leadership skills to improve how you handle tough conversations, communicate expectations, bring out the best in your team and hold people accountable

- Break through the mental blocks that cause you to procrastinate, overthink and doubt yourself, so that you can consistently take the actions you need to take

- Get you out of a reactive state so that you can stop, process problems and calmly respond to them, allowing you to feel more in control with less stress and anxiety

- Develop the right habits and routines to help you feel energized, stay focused, manage stress and feel your best inside and out

- Implement 'Ideal Life Creation' so that you can find balance, switch off, put the right boundaries in place and enjoy the success you worked so hard for

This is how I'm going to help you take control of your life and business, so that you can become the leader your business needs to take it to the next level of success.

The Evolved Method has been implemented by CEOs in 18 different countries by CEOs running everything from tech to SAAS and AI companies, real estate businesses, 7-figure agencies, financial institutions and billion-dollar unicorns in Silicon Valley.

Due to the high level of support in this program, joining is by application only. To apply for a place drop me an email at **byron@byronmorrison.com** and we can set up a call to see if working together is the right fit.

Alternatively, you can find out more at:

https://www.byronmorrison.com/evolved-program

What my clients have to say

On my website I have a section for client video case studies and testimonials sharing their thoughts from working together. You're welcome to go check them out in full at **www.byronmorrison.com**, but here are some extracts from what my clients had to say about working with me, after going through this Evolved transformation:

Cole (CEO): *"When something so transformative or someone so transformative enters your life it's really hard to put that impact in words right and that's that's how I felt about this entire experience working with you...As a Founder as a CEO as a person I could not more highly recommend working with Byron because it'll change your life, it's as simple as that. It couldn't be more of an honor or a pleasure to be able to call him a coach, a mentor a friend and a person you won't meet many people if any people in your life who are better human beings than this man is. So thank you Byron for everything that you've done everything you continue to do."*

Ron (CEO): *"After working with Byron and him offering the tools and rewiring my mindset, I have now come back as a more confident leader, I have learned how to defend my schedule, I've learned how to be less reactive, but to also to be able to just pause and look at situations and come up with a better plan, a better solution. I've set new standards...and I'm very confident that Byron is going to change your life for the better".*

Jordan (CEO): *"When I first started working with Byron, I really didn't feel like I was where I wanted to be. I felt like things were out of control, I didn't know how to get my life of working 80 hours and was struggling to spend enough time with my family. I was really trying to get that back, and what I found was that so much of what I didn't feel in control of, I had the ability to get in control of by changing the way I thought about things, by changing the way I approached situations, how present I was, having a true vision for my future, having action plan that really allowed me to recapture that control, to get organised, to come into meetings and be with my family, everything improved."*

Max (Tech CEO): *"Honestly, it's been one of the best decisions I've made. Certainly, compared to the financial investment the value that's come out of it has been astounding."*

Tyler (Business owner): *"I feel like I've left this universe and gone into a different one. It's been incredible...If you judge my level of happiness, clarity, sleep cycle, relationships, confidence, or every other area of my life, it's an easy win. My direction in life has completely changed".*

Rosemary (Business leader): *"I don't feel like I have control back, I feel like I have it for the first time. I used to be fighting all these fires and battles and it was exhausting. As everything felt out of my control and I was miserable. Now I feel calm and like that fire is merely a distraction that I know I can handle."*

Michael (CEO): *"I've gone from completely tired, exhausted, drained to back to my old self so to speak and with more purpose. I'm glad I did it, I certainly know that if I didn't, I'd probably still be in that state of unhappiness and stress. It was the best money I've ever spent on myself'.*

Neil (Business owner): *"I now feel completely different, I feel clear-headed and able to focus on the stuff I work out that I should be focusing on, I don't jump around anywhere near as much...I'm in control".*

Lauren (CEO): "You said you'd make me a better leader and you did. The time we've spent has been invaluable and our sessions are always exactly what I need to calibrate and process problems".

Josh (Business leader): *"People around me recognised that I'm more effective than I've ever been".*

Are you next?

Find out more and set up a time to speak directly to Byron to see if it is the right fit at:

https://www.byronmorrison.com/evolved-program

Summary

I know we've covered a lot, which is why I highly advise you take some to reflect on what we went through. Give yourself the time to figure out what principles you need to apply, changes you need to implement and how you can ensure you follow through with everything you need to do.

It will also no doubt be worth allowing some time for this new mentality to set in, then coming back and revisiting certain sections. After all, as you grow and evolve, you'll gain new perspectives and on a second read through you'll pick up new ideas and ways of thinking that you didn't before.

With that in mind, make sure you connect with and follow me on social media, as I regularly put out content based on the principles of this book and best practices I use with my clients.

LinkedIn:
https://www.linkedin.com/in/authorbyronmorrison/

Facebook:
https://www.facebook.com/byronmorrisonauthor/

Alternatively, drop me an email with any thoughts or questions at **byron@byronmorrison.com** and I'll personally respond.

Also make sure you check out my YouTube channel and "The Effective CEO" series. On here you'll find videos covering everything from figuring out what to delegate and prioritize to ways to defend your time, decision-making frameworks, energy management strategies, habits of highly effective CEOs, planning your day and so much more.

Watch now at **https://www.youtube.com/@ByronMorrison**

Leave a review

Like I wrote at the start of this book, my mission is to evolve CEOs into who they need to become to change the world. Which is why I believe that by getting them to take control of their role, they will be able to create a greater impact and change the lives of others for the better.

As with any mission though, I can't do it on my own. So if you enjoyed this book, it would mean the world to me if you'd take a moment to leave a review on Amazon to help spread the word.

Join our community

I believe that being part of a community and surrounding ourselves with the right people plays a vital role in our success. That's why as part of furthering my mission, I'm creating a community for impact-driven CEOs to meet others, find inspiration, share stories, and get support.

This is also going to be your go-to place to exchange ideas with other CEOs, share challenges, get support and continue your growth.

It's free to join, so if you haven't already you can join the community at:

https://www.facebook.com/groups/impactdrivenceos

Final thoughts

That's it, we've reached the end and I just want to say a huge thank you. I hope you enjoyed reading this book as much as I enjoyed writing it. If you want to dive more into the productivity side of performing at a higher level, then check out book 2 in the series "The Effective CEO". You can get a copy on Amazon.

If you have any questions about anything covered in this book feel free to get in touch at **byron@byronmorrison.com**.

Again, thanks for reading and whether we work together directly or cross paths in our community, I look forward to getting to know you better and finding more about your journey.

Byron Morrison

Made in the USA
Columbia, SC
21 November 2024